Cinco De Mayo: An Illustrated History

Roberto Cabello-Argandoña

Poetry Compiled, Edited and Translated

by Luis A. Torres

Floricanto™ Press

&

Berkeley Press

Cover: Acrilic Painting: Antonio González Orozco Juárez, Símbolo de la República, 1972, acrílico sobre madera

Floricanto™ Press
650 Castro Street, 120-331
Mountain View, California 94041
(415) 552-1879

ISBN: 978-1-888205-05-3

www.floricantopress.com

Floricanto Fress Series: Nuestra Histori a

Cinco de Mayo

Nuestra Historia Series

To Myriam Patricia for Her Adherence And Decades of Understanding and Moral Support.

Table of Contents

The Actors and the Battle Front

There is no social event, like an invasion, a war, or a battle, that does not have its leading actors--in both sides of the conflict-- who through their participation and actions ultimately determine the outcome of the armed conflict. What is so unique about these participants is that they were diametrically different from each other. For one, the invaders were Europeans from across the oceans in Europe with a different language, culture and technology, and political mind sets. The leading French and European participants were aristocrats, who held noble titles, from Emperor, Prince to Counts. On the other hand, the Mexican resistors were mostly all commoners, Mestizos and Indians, as Benito Juárez himself, and other generals. The European invaders believed that the best and only effective political system possible was monarchy. This view needs some pondering, because at that time most of the nations of the world, and all in Europe had some form monarchical government. The reader needs to take note that since the break-up of the Roma Empire in the Fifth Century, monarchy was the prevailing form of government in the western world, and otherwise. The United States had initiated a new and experimental form of republican government in the late 1700's, which influenced the choice of republican government of the newly formed nations that sprang from former colonies of the Spanish Empire in Latin America in the early 1800's. However, the United States in 1862 was engaged in a bitter civil war, and the Latin American republics, particularly Mexico, were also involved in civil strife, or had very unstable governments. Thus, it was not surprising that the Europeans would ponder about the virtues of a republican form of government and look down at the weakness of the political institutions in the Americas.

We have created in the following pages a gallery of the primary individuals participating in the conflict of Cinco de Mayo, as well as the geographical venue, where this battle took place. Most of the visual sources are paintings or drawings of the period found in Museums.

Mexican Defenders

"A LOS DEFENSORES DE PUEBLA DE ZARAGOZA,
EN 1862 Y 1863,
EL CONGRESO DE LA UNIÓN"
"TO THE DEFENDERS OF PUEBLA DE ZARAGOZA IN 1862 AND 1863,"
THE CONGRESS OF THE UNION"

"A Los Defensores de Puebla de Zaragoza, en 1862 y 1863." El Congreso de La Unión"

"To the Defenders of Puebla de Zaragoza in 1862 and 1863." The Congress of the Union.

Inscription in the Assembly Hall of the Mexican National Congress.

General Ignacio Zaragoza, Painting by Tejada, 1861.

In 1829, Ignacio Seguín Zaragoza was born outside the walls of the presidio de la Bahia. Ignacio Seguín Zaragoza became a general in the Mexican army. During the 1850s in Mexico Zaragoza sided with the liberal forces favoring the Plan de Ayutla, a political agreement among reformers to establish a republican government in Mexico. He took part in the battles of Saltillo and Monterey against the armies of Antonio López de Santa Anna.

On January 21, 1857, Ignacio Zaragoza married by proxy to Rafaela Padilla in Monterey. He was on an important army assignment in San Luis Potosí, was unable to attend his own marriage ; his brother, Miguel, served as his proxy.

Zaragoza and his wife had four children, three of whom died in infancy. During the War of the Reform (1857-60)--the struggle between conservative powers and liberal forces led by Benito Juárez-- Zaragoza sided with the liberals and took part in a number of military engagements. In 1857, during Comonfort's rebellion, Zaragoza led his army in the battle of Guadalajara, and in 1860 he participated in the battle of Calpulalpan, which ended the war. In April 1861 Juárez appointed Zaragoza minister of war and navy. Three months later President Juárez, overwhelmed by the losses of the civil war and attempting to gain control of the finances of Mexico, declared a two-year moratorium on Mexico's European debts. In December a fleet of Spanish ships stationed in Cuba arrived at Veracruz and forced the surrender of the city. This invasion was followed by France and England, as they joined the Spanish navy.

Zaragoza resigned from the ministry to lead the Army of the East in defense of Mexico, and in February 1862, a month after his wife's death in Mexico City, he began work on the defenses of Puebla in preparation of the Battle of Puebla. Early in 1862 the English and Spanish withdrew; French forces attacked Puebla in a battle that lasted the entire day of May 5, 1862, the now-famed Cinco de Mayo. Zaragoza's well-armed, well-trained men forced the withdrawal of the French troops from Puebla to Orizaba.

In mid-August of 1862 Zaragoza went to Mexico City, where he was received as a hero. When he returned to Puebla he became ill with typhoid fever and died there on September 8, 1862. A state funeral was held in Mexico City and he was laid to rest at the Panteón de San Fernando. On September 11, 1862, President Juárez issued a decree changing the name of the city of Puebla de los Angeles to Puebla de Zaragoza and making Cinco de Mayo a national holiday. Zaragoza became one of the great national heroes of Mexico. Cinco de Mayo today is celebrated both in Mexico and United States.

Statue of General Ignacio Zaragoza, Presidio Nuestra Señora de Loreto de La Bahia, Goliad, Texas.

Statue in Goliad of General Ignacio Zaragoza. The background depicts El Presidio de la Bahia and the birthplace of General Zaragoza . In the 1960s General Zaragoza State Historic Site was established near Goliad to commemorate Zaragoza's birthplace. In 1980 dignitaries from the United States, Texas, and Mexico participated in the dedication of a ten-foot bronze statue honoring Zaragoza, commissioned by Alfredo Toxqui Fernández de Lara, governor of Puebla, as a gift to the people of Goliad and Texas.

General Ignacio Zaragoza, Oil on cardboard by Tejada, 1861.

Ignacio Zaragoza, oil canvas, unknown, XIX Century.

General Ignacio Zaragoza addressed the Mexican defenders before the Battle of Puebla on Cinco de Mayo, May Fifth, 1862:

"Your enemies are the first soldiers of the world, but you are the first sons of Mexico. They wish to seize your Fatherland. Soldiers! I read victory and faith on your foreheads, Long Live Independence! Long live the Fatherland!"

Ignacio Zaragoza

Oil Canvas by Rafael Aguirre, 1898

¡Las armas nacionales se han cubierto de gloria!

The national arms are covered in glory!

Ignacio Zaragoza proclaimed victory over the French forces in the Battle of Puebla on May 5, 1862, in a message to President Benito Juárez. This battle is commemorated on the 500-peso bill.

Benito Juârez and his wife, Margarita Maza de Juárez. Oil on canvas by José Escudero y Espronceda, 1890.

Benito Juárez

Oil canvas by Pelegrín Clavé, 1863

Benito Pablo Juárez García, (1806-1872), was born March 21, 1806, , in the state of Oaxaca, Mexico, in the town of San Pablo Gueletao. Benito Juárez was a Zapotec Indian who at the age of 13 could not read or write Spanish. In Oaxaca he benefitted from from the educational opportunities available, and graduated from the Franciscan seminary in 1827, and later became a city councilman in 1831-1833. In 1834 he graduated from Oaxaca's Institute of Science and Art with a degree in law, and became a judge in 1841, and later became a member of the Supreme Court of Justice of the nation. He served a term as a federal deputy and served as governor of the state of Oaxaca in 1846-1852.

In 1853 many liberals were exiled, including Juárez, who spent his time of exile in New Orleans when the conservatives took power in Mexico. Benito Juárez returned from his exile as the Minister of Justice in 1855 when the liberals won the election.

In 1857 he was appointed to preside over the supreme court, becoming in effect the Vice President. In 1858 Juárez had to leave again Mexico City, this time to Veracruz, where he created a government in exilet, as a result of conservative rebellion .

The conservatives lost power and the civil war in January 1861 , and Benito Juárez was elected the President of Mexico. As Mexico was practically in financial ruin after years of civil strife, Juárez made the decision to suspend payment of all foreign debts for a two year period. Juarez attempted to re-negotiate the debt, but the Mexican congress rejected the agreement Juárez had made with the British Prime Minister to protect the interests of European countries. The Spanish navy, which had war ships stationed in Cuba, flollowed by British and French troops landed in Vera Cruz. Spain and Britain were there to protect their financial interests, and left in April, after they received assurances of repayment and it became clear that France had conquest in mind. The French troops fought for two years, and although suffering a serious defeat on 5th May 1862, eventually captured Mexico City in June 1863, and placed Archduke Maximilian of Austria on the Mexican throne.

Benito Juarez and the government of Mexico were forced to retreat right back to Ciudad Juarez, on the border with the USA. After four years with growing pressure from America, continuing resistance from Mexicans and criticism from the French govenrment and people, finally the Napoleonic forces withdrew.

Maximilian himself was captured and executed on 19th June 1867.

Juarez returned to Mexico city, and the presidency even after suffering a stroke in October 1870, and the loss of his wife in 1871. He won the presidential election in 1871, but died on 18th July 1872, of a heart attack.

Benito Juárez

Oil on canvas by Pelegrín Clavé, 1862

General José de la Cruz Porfirio Díaz Mori (1830-1915) was born September 16, 1830 in Oaxaca. He worked as a youngster as a shoe-maker to help support his widowed mother. He attended the Franciscan seminary in Oaxaca and graduated from law at the Institute of Science and Art of Oaxaca. Díaz joined the Mexican National Guard in 1846 to fight against the United States in the Mexican American War (1846-1848). Díaz was forced into exile by president Antonio López de Santa Anna and was instrumental in the overthrow of Santa Anna. He distinguished himself in the War of the Reform (1857-1860), and fought at the Battle of Puebla and elsewhere until the Mexicans prevailed against the French invaders. He inflicted nine defeats on the imperialist forces, was twice wounded in combat, escaped capture three times, but surrendered once. When Díaz returned 87,232 pesos of unspent funds earmarked for the offensive against Maximilian, he gained a reputation of integrity.

Porfirio Díaz, Oil canvas by José Obregón, 1883

Gen. Juan Francisco Lucas

One that gave fame to the Zacapoaxtian Indian soldiers because in this battle fought three men of the same first names: Juan N. Méndez, Juan Crisóstomo Bonilla and Juan Francisco Lucas. They are known as "The Three Johns."

Gen. Miguel Eliecer Negrete

Chief of the Firing Line between the Loreto and Guadalupe Fortresses. He showed a singular bravery when at the face of the enemy, who was finally sent away defeated.

General Felipe B. Berriozábal (1829-1900) was born in Zacatecas in 1829. He studied at the National Engineering School in Mexico City, and later joined the army as an officer. As a lieutenant, he fought against the United States in the Mexican War of 1846-1847. He sided with the Liberals during the War of the Reform. He served as the provisional governor of the federal district of Mexico City between 1857 and 1862. Berriozábal's most distinguished milestone was to have commanded an infantry brigade of regular soldiers and Mexican volunteers at the battle of Puebla on May 5, 1862. In 1863 he served as Mexican Minister of War and the Navy in the government of Benito Juárez, and was governor of the state of Michoacán from late 1863 to 1864.

In 1876, Berriozábal was named Minister of War, during the interim government of President José María Iglesias Inzaurraga. During the administration of President Porfirio Díaz he occupied several ministerial positions, he was Minister of Government, and later, Minister of War and the Navy. After a long and distinguished career, he died at Mexico City on January 9, 1900.

General Tomás O'Haran y Escudero. Oil on canvas, unknown, XIX Century.

General Ignacio Mejía, Aide de Camp of General Ignacio Zaragoza at the memorable battle of Cinco de Mayo. Oil canvas, unknown.

General Félix Díaz.

Oil canvas, José Escudero y Espronceda, 1890.

Félix Díaz, *a liuetenant, was the younger brother of General Porfirio Díaz. He commanded a provisional regiment of cavalry, consisting of squadrons of lancers from the cities of Oaxaca and Toluca, at the battle of Puebla in 1862.*

General Félix María Zuloaga Trillo *(1814-1876) was born in the town of Los Alamos in the state of Chihuahua. After joining the Mexican Army as a National Guard Lieutenant in 1824, he fought against the Apache Indians on the northern frontier until 1837. Then he joined the Corps of Engineers and continued to serve in the Army through the riots of 1840 and the Yucatan insurgency of 1842-1843. He retired as a Lieutenant-Colonel.*

Sebastián Lerdo de Tejada y Corral, (1825-1889), was born in Jalapa April 25, 1825, Lerdo was educated as a lawyer. He was a leader in the Liberal party and a strong supporter of President Juárez. Lerdo served as a member of the Supreme Court of Mexico, was Mexico's Minister of Foreign Affairs in 1857, and became president of the Chamber of Deputies in 1861. During the French intervention he again served as Foreign Minister in the Juárez government. When Juárez died in 1872 Lerdo succeeded him in office. Lerdo was reelected to the presidency on July 24,1876. but was overthrown in a coup led by Porfirio Díaz in January of 1877. He fled to the United States and died in obscurity at New York in 1889.

The Mexican Conservatives supporters of the French Intervention

(Two of these generals were executed with Emperor Maximilian.)

Conservative General Juan Nepomuceno Almonte.

Oil canvas, Ortega, 1854.

Almonte was an illegitimate son of a mestizo parish priest--José María Morelos y Pavón, a guerilla leader and revolutionary who fought for the independence of Mexico from Spain--and an Indian woman Brígida Almonte. He was born in Necupétaro, Michoacán on 15 May 1803.

Almonte lived and studied several years inthe United States, in New Orleans. He had a prominent career. He occupied many important posts, such as Secretary and Advisor to General Santa Anna. ; In 1840 Almonte became Minister of War under ***Anastacio Bustamante***, and was instrumental in suppressing a rebellion initiated by General José Urrea. After Bustamente was overthrown, Almonte was foced to support lecturing.

General Almonte participated in the battles of the Alamo and San Jacinto. His biographical notes in preparation to the Battle of the Alamo are a significant primary source for the study of the period. After Santa Anna returned to power, Almonte was appointed Minister to the United States. When the U.S. Congress passed the bill for the annexation of Texas, Almonte denounced it, stating *"that America had committed the most unjust act recorded in history."*

Almonte was Minister to Great Britain in 1846; 1853 to the United States; 1856 again to Great Britain. While in Europe and in contrast to his earlier nationalistic positions, Almonte helped to engineer the European intervention in Mexico and promoted the return of Mexico to monarchy. He returned to from Paris to Mexioc with the French troops in 1862. He was appointed "supreme chief" of Mexico by the French and president of the French Executive Council that brought in emperor Maximilian. Almonte died 21 Mar 1869 in Paris while envoy to France appointed by the emperor.

General Tómás Mejía, 1815-1867, was born in the town of Sierra Gorda in the state of Guanajuato state in about 1815, Mejia was a pureblooded Indian. He was an ardent defender of the Catholic Church, and after the overthrow of the dictatorship of General Antonio Lopez de Santa Anna in 1855, he began raising his fellow Indians to fight against the new Liberal regime. He distinguished himself as a capable military leader during the War of the Reform (1857-1860). When the Conservative forces were defeated, Mejia and his men retreated into the mountains to continue the fight.

When the French invaded Mexico and promised to restore the Conservative party to power, Mejia joined them. He won a series of victories as military commander in northeastern Mexico, gaining a reputation for fighting skill and for the humane treatment of his captives. He and his troops joined Emperor Maximilian at Queretaro, and when that city fell, he was captured by the Liberal forces of Benito Juárez. Mejia put on trial by a military court, convicted of various war crimes, and sentenced to death by firing squad. He was executed at Queretaro on June 19, 1867, along with Emperor Maximilian and General Miguel Miramón.

General Miguel Miramón [Miguel Gregorio de la Luz Atenógenes Miramón y Tarelo] (1832-1867) was born at Mexico City on September 29, 1832. Miramón took part as a cadet in the unsuccessful military defenses against United States troops during the Mexican War in 1847 at Molino del Rey and the Military Academy at Chapultepec. He was wounded in battle, captured and released after the Treaty of Guadalupe Hidalgo ended the Mexican American War. Miramón completed his studies at the Chapultepec Military Academy and joined the Army in 1852 to fight fight on the side of the Conservative party during the War of the Reform (1857-1860). He rose to a leadership position, and was named president of Mexico, replacing Félix Zuloaga in January 1859. Miramón fled into exile after his forces were totally defeated on December 22, 1860 at the battle of Calpulalpam. This battle effectively ended the War of the Reform, leaving Benito Juárez and his Liberal party of as rulers of Mexico.

Miramón, in November of 1866, was commanding a division in the Imperial Mexican Army of the Emperor Maximilian. Miramón was forced to withdraw to Queretaro after his troops were defeated in the battle of San Jacinto on February 1, 1867 by the Juarista General Mariano Escobedo. After a siege, the city of Queretaro was taken by the forces of Juárez, who captured Miramón, General Tomas Mejia and Emperor Maximilian. All three were put on trial by a military court, convicted , and sentenced to death by firing squad. Miramón was executed at Queretaro on June 19, 1867.

The French Invaders

Napoleon III [Charles Louis Napoléon Bonaparte] (1808-1873) was born April 21, 1808 in Paris, he was the son of Louis Bonaparte, king of Holland 1806-1810, and Hortense de Beauharnais. As the nephew of **Napoléon Bonaparte**, Louis Napoleon believed that he was the rightful heir to the French throne. In 1836 he attempted an unsuccessful coup d'état and fled to New York. He later returned to France and tried a second unsuccessful coup d'état; he was captured and sentenced to life in prison. Bonaparte escaped in May, 1846 and took refuge in London. He returned to Paris during the upheaval of the French revolution of 1848, and managed to get elected to a seat in the French parliament.

In December of 1848, he was elected President of France. The French constitution imposed single term limits to all office holders, and after an attempt to amend the constitution failed in July of 1851, Louis Napoleon engineered a coup which overthrew the government that December. A new French constitution was drafted in January, 1852, which gave Bonaparte powers to rule by decree, thus becoming a dictator. In November of that year he appointed himself

Napoleon III, emperor of the French.

Napoleon was obssesed with expanding French prestige in Europe and the world. Under his regime France allied itself with Great Britain to fight the Crimean War in 1854-1856 against Russia, and later to fight a war against China in 1857-1860. Napoleon seized Indochina and fought to end Austrian influence in Italy in 1859.

When in 1861 Mexico was forced to suspend payments on its foreign debts, Napoleon III plotted to carve out a French empire in Mexico. France allied with Great Britain and Spain landed an expeditionary force at Vera Cruz. Mexican president Benito Juárez promised to see that the debts were paid and Great Britain and Spain withdrew . The French, however, having greater designs marched on Mexico City. The invading French forces were defeated at the battle of Puebla (May 5, 1862), setting back Napoleon III's plans for a year.

Napoleon III, Emperor of the French (Chateau de Versailles)

Napoleon, III . Oil on canvas Pelegrí Clavé, 1860

Napoleon, III (Le Petit).

Oil on canvas, Pelegrín Clavé, 1860.

Empress Carlotta of Mexico, Princess Charlotte-Amelie of Belgium, (1840-1927) was the daughter of King Leopold I of Belgium. In 1857, when she was 17, she married Archduke Maximilian, who served as Viceroy of Lombardy in 1859-1861. This portrait shows her dressed in the formal national costume of Lombardy. A decisive and smart woman, she helped Maximilian to reign Mexico. She went to Europe in 1866 to get financial assistance and support for the disintegrating Empire of Mexico. After Maximilian's execution in 1867, she became ill and reportdely became mad. Finally passing away at 86 years of age in Belgium in 1927.

Archduke Ferdinand Maximilian Josef von Habsburg [Maximilian] (1832-1867) was born July 6, 1832 at Schoenbrunn castle in Austria. Maximilian was the younger brother of Emperor Franz Josef of Austria-Hungary. In this engraving, he is shown wearing the uniform of an Admiral of the Fleet of the Austro-Hungarian Navy. Napoleon III, to gain the support of Franz Josef, selected Maximilian to head the French Imperial government of Mexico in 1862. He and his wife Charlotte (Carlota), daughter of King Leopold of Belgium, traveled to Mexico to take possession of Empire. However, when the Mexican adventure of Napoleon III collapsed in 1867, Maximilian was captured and executed by a Mexican firing squad by orders of Benito Juárez..

Empress Charlotte Emily Von Hapsburg.

Oil Canvas by Albert Graefle, 1860.

Emperor Maximilian. Oil canvas, Albert Graefle, 1860.

Carlotta, Empress of Mexico (Museum of History, Chapultepec)

Charles Ferdinand Latrille, Count de Lorencez

Charles Ferdinand Latrille, Count de Lorencez, Commanding French General of the French invading army, was born in Paris, May 23, 1814. He graduated from the military school of Saint Cyr in 1830 as a 3rd lieutenant. He served as a colonel in Algiers in 1852 . During the Crimean war was elevated to the position of major-general in 1855 with the capture of the Malakoff. , He was sent to Mexico in January, 1862 with re-enforcements for the expedition that had landed earlier in December, 1861. He arrived at Vera Cruz on 5 March, and was made lieutenant-general on the 20th. He left the camp of Chiquihuite on 19 April, and on the following morning entered Orizaba, after defeating some Mexican forces in a cavalry engagement. On the 23rd of April he was joined by the Mexican General Galvez with a force of volunteers. Lorencez took command of the French forces in Mexico on April, 27th He defeated the patriots at Acultzingo on 28 April, entered Amozoc on May 4th, and on the following day on Cinco de Mayo attacked the fortified hills of Guadalupe and Loreto at Puebla. The lack of proper artillery, made him impossible to capture these forts, and retreated toward Orizaba. He crossed the Cumbres heights on the 16th, and on the following morning was joined at Tecomolucan by an insurgent chief Marquez and his 500 cavalry contingent. Zaragoza was beaten after a sharp action at Acultzingo on 18 May, and on the 20th Lorencez arrived at Orizaba, which he fortified, as he had resolved to await the arrival of re-enforcements in that city. On 17 June he defeated

Zaragoza again, but the French forces suffered heavily from yellow fever and want of provisions.

Later Napoleon III sent a larger army to Mexico, but placed Lorencez second in command under General Forey. Lorencez asked to be recalled, and left Vera Cruz on 17 December, 1862. General Lorencez became a vocal opponent of the French Imperial ambitions in Mexico; he opposed sending of reinforcements to Mexico, urging the emperor to recall his troops, and predicting that the war would be disastrous. He fought during the Franco-German war of 1870s, but a disease contracted in Mexico compelled him to retire from active service in 1872.

The Battle Front

The Spanish Navy at the Port of Veracruz, The first naval contingent of the Alliance to invade Mexico.

The French Imperial Army camped at Amozoc, outside Puebla.

La Iglesia de Los Remedios, Military Headquarters of General Ignacio Zaragoza and the Mexican Army of East.

The Battle of Puebla. A Mexican cavalryman engaging a French soldier.

Death of Zouave *(Bello Museum, Puebla, Mexico.) This painting depicts a Mexican irregular attacking a French Zouave. A XIX century oil painting, unknown.*

A closer view of the Battle of Puebla. Painting. Unknown.

Engraving of the battle of Puebla, May 5, 1862, showing the French attack with Fort Guadalupe in the distance

The defeated French forces shown decimated and unable to seize the Forts of Loreto and Guadalupe at the Battle of Puebla on Cinco de Mayo. Oil painting, unknown.

A Zuoave in uniform; oil painting at the Galilean Library.

On May 15, 1867, Maximilian surrendered to General Mariano Escobedo. A month later, Maximilian was executed, ending — once and for all — French occupation of Mexico.

Cinco de Mayo: History

Introduction

by Antonio Ríos Bustamante

and Luis Leobardo Arroyo

This monograph provides information about the historical context and examines 19th century poetry by Mexicans in the United States celebrating the battle of Cinco de Mayo and the particulars of General Ignacio Zaragoza and his troops' victory over the French army at the City of Puebla on that day of 1862. This book intends to satisfy the curiosity of the growing number of persons who may be familiar with the history of Cinco de Mayo and wish to learn why and how the holiday is celebrated in Mexico and the United States. The book is divided into two parts. Part I examines briefly the historical background to the French Intervention in Mexico and the Battle of Puebla. That era's political history provided the context for politically-conservative Mexicans turning to Napoleon III, Emperor of France, and beseeching him to overthrow the liberal government of President Benito Juárez. It discusses with details the arrival of General Charles Francois Latrille, Count of Lorencez, and his troops at Veracruz and their subsequent march on Mexico City. It also describes the Mexican army's and the general population's mobilization, led General Zaragoza, to engage and stop the French army in battle at the City of

Puebla. To everyone's great surprise, the Mexicans beat the world's greatest military power.

Zaragoza's victory was so improbable and unexpected that it stimulated feelings of pride, nationalism, and determination to defend Mexico's sovereignty in the hearts of many Mexicans who previously had shown little interest in the future of their country. The cry of ¡Viva el Cinco de Mayo! was to inspire increasing numbers of Mexicans to come to the aid of their country during the years 1863 to1867. For although the Mexicans had won the Battle of Puebla on Cinco de Mayo 1862, a year later the French military juggernaught had nonetheless overwhelmed the government of President Benito Juárez. Urged on by exiled conservative Mexicans in Paris, Napoleon III approved the establishment of a monarchy for Mexico and convinced Archduke Maximilian Ferdinand Joseph of Austria to become the new Emperor of Mexico.

Maximilian's reign was based on the largesse of French financial assistance and the superiority of the French army over the Mexican military and guerrillas that had rallied to the support of the government of President Juárez. With the withdrawal of French troops to Europe in late 1866 and early 1867, however, Maximilian and his conservative Mexican supporters proved no match for President Juárez and his republican army. On the 19th of June 1867, Maximilian and several of his Mexican military officers were executed by firings quad near the city of Querétaro. Thus ended French imperial ambitions in Mexico; thus Mexico regained its freedom and sovereignty.

Part II is a collection of patriotic poems which appeared in El Nuevo Mundo, a newspaper published in San Francisco, California on the Cinco Mayo and the events relating to the French Intervention in Mexico. These poems and the events relating to the French intervention in Mexico. These poems were collected, edited and translated into English by Luis Torres as part of a larger work entitled The World of Early Chicano Poetry, 1846-1910 published by Floricanto Press.

Cinco de Mayo in the late nineteenth-century served not only to enkindle Mexican patriotism but as well to engender popular support for the Mexican government and in particular one of its leaders, Porfirio Díaz who had a leading role in the Battle of Puebla of 1862, and erstwhile dictator of the Republic from 1876 to 1911.During the late nineteenth-century, Cinco de Mayo was celebrated by Mexican Americans living in the lands that Mexico had lost to the United States because of the Texas Revolt of 1836 and the Mexican American War of 1846-1848.For these Mexican Americans, experiencing sharp dislocations and privations in their private and public lives at the hands of White Americans, Cinco de Mayo took on significance as an example of Mexicans defending themselves successfully from foreign invasion; it provided the opportunity to express public pride in their culture and to celebrate their determination to resist the imposition of American rule. With the advent of the Chicano Movement in the mid-1960s, Cinco de Mayo celebrations took on additional meanings. They provided opportunities for Mexican Americans to express their pride in their Mexican heritage and as well to proclaim the beauty and importance of Chicano culture to the larger society. Greater tolerance and commerce have contributed to spread in the United States the celebration of Cinco de Mayo in institutions and organizations throughout.

Preface

Antonio Ríos-Bustamante and Luis Leobardo Arroyo

El Cinco de Mayo, the Fifth of May, is a Mexican holiday heavily loaded with many layers of symbolism. This symbolism ranges from the festive carnival atmosphere found in restaurant and bar celebrations, to expressions of patriotism and nationalism characteristic of parades and civic commemorations, to public speeches and political tracts articulating the perennial importance of the inviolability of the nation's sovereignty, the people's right to self determination, and opposition to foreign intervention. We may gain some insight into why these principles have come to be associated with Cinco de Mayo by briefly examining what occurred that day in 1862 against the backdrop of Mexico's political history. The events leading to the Battle at Puebla of May 5, 1862 (La Batalla de Puebla) took shape in the aftermath of the Mexican American War of 1846-48. Crushed by the United States military and forced to forfeit half the National territory to the conquerors, Mexico entered a period of National crisis during the 1850s. Self-styled liberals and conservatives initially clashed over whose leaders and policies could restore political stability and bring economic prosperity to the nation. But their struggles erupted into civil war. Beginning in 1858, the War of the Reform, pitted the liberal government against the onslaughts of pro-clerical conservatives and their armies. By January 1861 the government of President Benito Juárez bad defeated its conservative enemies. But years of warfare had left the country devastated and bankrupt. In July 1861, Juárez suspended payments on the foreign debt for two years. His action angered the principal creditor countries, France, Britain and Spain. They organized a military expedition that occupied the port city of Veracruz and seized the custom receipts in order to pay the monies Mexico owed their respective citizens. Within months, Britain and Spain achieved through negotiations their objectives and withdrew. Emperor Napoleon III, on the other hand, refused to withdraw France's troops; for his plan was to organize a protectorate in Mexico, similar to the one in Indochina, and thereby re-establish the French empire in the Americas.

The Juárez government faced a seemingly hopeless situation in preparing to defend the country. The French army was reputedly the greatest military power in the world, and rallying to the assistance of Napoleon III were many conservative Mexicans and Catholic bishops who were eager for one more opportunity to oust the liberals from power. En spite of the odds against them, the Mexican government, nonetheless, prepared to fight; its troops buoyed by a renewed sense of nationalism and confidence from their victory in the War of the Reform, its officers inspired by love of country and the unwavering leadership of Juárez.

The Battle of Puebla took place on el Cinco de Mayo 1862. A French army of 6,500 veteran troops, under the command of General Latrille, Count of Lorencez, was marching from Veracruz to Mexico City; traveling along the road of conquest carved out by Hernán Cortés and his conquistadores in 1519; the same road followed by General Winfield Scott and his troops in 1847 during the Mexican American War. Although the city of Puebla was a conservative and proclerical stronghold, several forts stood between the city and the approaching French army. There General Ignacio Zaragoza, in command of less of 5,000 militia and army regulars, chose to engage the enemy. Ignacio Zaragoza was an extraordinary person. Born in La Bahía de Espíritu Santo in the Mexican state of Texas, he had experienced firsthand the humiliation of defeat, when his family had fled its ancestral home during the Texas Revolt of 1836. With the outbreak of the War of the Reform, Zaragoza volunteered to serve in the militia. He quickly demonstrated a rare blend of political idealism and talent for commanding troops while under fire. These qualities accounted for his rapid promotion to the rank of general. He proved to be an excellent field commander in the liberals stunning defeat of the conservatives at Silao and recapture of the city of Guadalajara in 1860. He would exhibit the same leadership talents at Puebla. Before engaging the French, Zaragoza exhorted his soldiers to remember: "Your enemies are the first soldiers in the World, but you are the first Sons of Mexico. They have come to take your country from you." The Mexican defenders took their leader's words to heart. Taking advantage of several tactical mistakes by General Charles

Latrille, and of the weakened condition of many French troops who were too sick to fight effectively, Mexican troops repulsed several attacks on their positions. Savage hand to hand fighting broke the back of several French assaults. The Mexican victory was assured when the Second Brigade, under the command of Brigadier General Porfirio Díaz, executed flawlessly Zaragoza's ordered counterattack against a major French offensive late in the afternoon. Much to the chagrin of the French minister to Mexico City and his proclerical and conservative Mexican supporters, Latrille withdrew from the field of battle. Liberal Mexicans had won the day.

The victory at Puebla delayed the French advance on Mexico City for one year. While the French army awaited reinforcements and a propitious time to renew its advance on Mexico City, Juárez laid the groundwork for an ongoing war against Napoleon III and his cronies. Once the French had forced Juárez to flee the capital city and proceeded to install Maximilian as Emperor of Mexico, Cinco de Mayo took on added significance. It served not only as a reminder that Mexicans had earlier defeated their conquerors; Cinco de Mayo also became a much needed symbol of Mexican resistance to foreign domination and action on behalf of National sovereignty. With the reestablishment of Mexican independence in 1867, Cinco de Mayo took on international significance, becoming a symbol of self determination and sovereignty for oppressed peoples everywhere. The defeat of Cinco de Mayo would haunt the French Imperial Army for years to come. Evidence of the universal significance of Cinco de Mayo can be found in the anguished cries of French citizens upon learning of the Prussians victory over the French army at the battle at Metz in 1877: "Why did you not do as the Mexicans at Puebla?" They demanded to know of their fallen Emperor Napoleon III and his leading officer, General Bazaine. El Cinco de Mayo also has an enduring significance for the Mexican people in the United States. During the 1860s the struggle of the legitimate Mexican government of President Juárez inspired wide support among Mexicanos in the Southwest. In California, the Nevada mining camps, and elsewhere, Mexicans and Mexican Americans formed Clubes Liberales (liberal clubs) or Juntas Patrióticas de Juárez. These organizations raised money and sent men and weapons to aid the Juárez government in its war against Emperor Maximilian and his French troops.

In Texas, Nuevo Leon and Tamaulipas, General Nepomuceno Cortina led a guerilla army against the French military, Mexican conservative armies, and the Texan Confederates alike. Cinco de Mayo, like the battles of Britain and Stalingrad in World War II, became a symbol of determined resistance to aggression. In the early twentieth century, the Battle at Puebla on Cinco de Mayo and the declaration of Mexican independence on September 16 were the major holidays and symbols of la Raza Mexicana, the Mexican people, in both Mexico and the United States. Since the end of World War II, however, Cinco de Mayo has waned in importance in Mexico, and is at best a minor holiday, particularly in comparison to the celebration of

Mexican Independence. In contrast, Cinco de Mayo remains an important holiday for la raza Mexicana in the United States; since the 1970s, there is even some evidence that suggests the popularity of Cinco de Mayo has come to exceed Mexican Independence Day. As celebrated by the Mexican people in the United States, Cinco de Mayo symbolizes our pride in our Mexican identity and our aspirations for the well-being, dignity and future advance of Mexico and of la raza Mexicana, the Mexican people north of the Rio Bravo, and all people everywhere. From the 1860s to the 1990s, the symbolic importance of Cinco de Mayo remains significant to the nations of Latin America and the Third World as they face the crushing weight of immense foreign debts and bitter conflicts which threaten world peace. To this day Mexican foreign policy embodies a key principle associated with Cinco de Mayo: opposition to foreign intervention in the internal affairs of nations. As Benito Juárez once said: "Respeto a los derechos ajenos es la paz." Peace is the respect of other people's rights.

Part I

Prologue

Una Casa En Conflicto. A House in Conflict

Cinco de Mayo has been celebrated in Mexico and the United States since 1863 in commemoration of La Batalla de Puebla (The Battle of Puebla) in 1862 in which a smaller contingent of Mexican regulars and civilians defeated a larger, battle-trained French invading force at La Ciudad de Puebla de Los Angeles (City of Puebla). Indeed, there have been many battles at Puebla, but, during the French Invasion of Mexico, two are especially significant.

The first battle was on May Fifth, 1862, which is the subject of this book. The second one is known as El Sitio de Puebla (The Siege of Puebla) which went from March 17th through May 17th, 1863. Therefore, Mexican patriots clashed twice with French troops in Puebla on May Fifth, 1862 and 1863. As scholars and historians devote more energies to study and research the events leading to and surrounding Cinco de Mayo, 1862, it is edifying to know that historical evidence so far indicates that celebrations of this event were held in the United States by Mexican Americans as early as 1864, only two years after the Cinco de Mayo battle of 1862.

What causes led to the invasion of Mexico by a distant European power? What foreign policy objectives was France attempting to achieve? What impact would this bellicose action have on neighboring countries, such as the United States? More precisely, What were the risks of this invasion for France, in light of American foreign policy pronouncements? How would the United States would react to the European threat in the American continent, considering that the Monroe Doctrine set America, the New World, outside European influence? More importantly, How would Mexicans view this invasion and respond to it? How would Mexicans living in the United States and Mexican Americans would react to foreign troops marching on Mexican soil?

The French Invasion of Mexico and the circumstances that led to the encounter on Cinco de Mayo, 1862 were rooted on the complex history of Mexico, as well as, factors impinging upon international relations among world powers. The latter encompasses geopolitical ambitions and economic considerations at the time among the dominant world powers: England, France, Spain, and the Austrian Empire sought to expand their influence in to the Americas and, possibly challenge the United States.

The occurrence of the Battle of Puebla was also imbedded in the complex local history of Mexico and the emerging notions of nationalism ("*lo Mexicano*"), after its independence from Spain. Mexican history, during this period, was characterized by its political search for a new representative form of government, which was burdened by deep internal divisions, further afflicted by a collapsed economy, and plagued by foreign threats against Mexico's newly acquired sovereignty.

Mexico: The Crown Jewel of the Spanish Empire

New Spain, as Mexico was known during the Spanish colonial period, was a rare gem in the Spanish Crown. Mexico was rich in exports of silver, tobacco, agricultural products, textiles, cotton, ceramics and artisanship. During the decade of preindependence, the annual value of agricultural production, mining, and manufacturing reached to 200 million pesos. The annual production of silver alone reached to 30 million pesos. The Crown's annual receipts were estimated at 70 million pesos. Mexico enjoyed a rich cultural life by any standards. Educational establishments, newspapers, literature and the arts flourished as they were underwritten by a strong trade, export economy, and European imports, ideas and culture. At the time, Spain was also known as the Peninsula Ibérica, and Mexico's colonial society was characterized by a peninsular dominated mercantilist economy and a peninsular gentry. Mexico traded mostly with Spain. Mexican silver and gold found its way to Spanish coffers, enriching both the Crown and the local Peninsular elite. This aristocracy was comprised of Spaniards who enjoyed great wealth through official royal appointments in the administration of the colony, large (grant) landholdings and mining concerns. The peninsulares were also known pejoratively as gachupines. The criollos, on the other hand, were native-born descendants of peninsulares, who generally lacked the royal benefits of position and wealth. Their interests and emotions were rooted in Mexico, and in the end they came to challenge the colonial government. Mestizos were descendants of the intermarriage between criollos or peninsulares and indios. The alliance criollo-mestizo had to struggle for positions in the colonial government and social recognition in colonial society. The Indians and mulattos-descendants of black slaves-were at the margin of this prosperous society. The criollo-mestizo sectors had to use skills as opposed to privileges to advance themselves; they became students, junior officers, clerics, intellectuals, shop-owners, small farmers, and miners and developed their own popular nativist culture which was Mexican, rather than European or Spanish.

These groups formed the basis of the castas, or caste system, that maintained a different social and economic position for each group, although they shared a common veneration for the Catholic Church and loyalty to the Spanish Crown. Spain and Mexico, as it was with all the colonies, had only one source of legitimate authority and power, the King. The Spanish Monarchy was the only political and ideological bond that existed between the colonies and Spain. Mexicans owed not loyalty to Spain itself, but the Crown. As we shall see, European political events were going to change that relationship substantially.

As popular uprisings in Paris culminated into the full fledged French Revolution (1789), and eventually overturned the French Monarchy and the landed gentry, its ideological and political impact swept throughout Europe. Napoleon Bonaparte eventually succeeded in filling the vacuum left by the monarchy and began a French expansionist movement that in the end tumbled the Spanish Bourbon Monarchy of Ferdinand VII and substituted his rule by that of his brother, José Bonaparte (Pepe Botella) as King of Spain and all the colonies.

This imperial plight became a crisis of authority and grew into a political dispute which opened the door for Mexican demands for independence from Spain. This call for independence from the outset was more anti-French than anti-Spanish. It was a demand against the Napoleonic usurpers of the Spanish crown. It also entailed a first step toward Mexicanismo. In other words, New Spain, without a legitimate Spanish king, had to search and find its own self, as a separate entity from Spain. Its was indeed a first step toward nationalism, *lo mexicano*.

Cinco de Mayo:

Mexico's Independence and Internal Conflict

The Battle of Cinco de Mayo of 1862 was largely a consequence of unresolved political issues and domestic antagonisms originating from Mexico's Independence. At the eve of their independence, Mexicans of all walks of life had a common purpose, breaking away from Spain, and a common enemy, the peninsulares. However, once Mexico achieved independence from Spain, the various castes and pressure groups, who were allied against Spain, became competitors for power and, eventually, bitter enemies. These factions in time, held different competing visions of and for Mexico, as they attempted to shape policy and maximize their positions. The acrimony among social groups led to conflict and civil war, and, ultimately, to the European Intervention of Mexico.

The cries for independence initiated by Father Miguel Hidalgo y Costilla on September 16, 1810-!Viva el Rey! Long live the King!-were articulated as a support to the House of Bourbon and King Ferdinand VII who had been overthrown by Napoleon the I. The cries were also expressions of deep hatred against the peninsulares and their odious rule: ¡Muerte a los gachupines! Death to the Gachupines! The usurpation of the throne by José Bonaparte had created a political and ideological crisis of authority.

If the legitimate Spanish King was gone, Who was to rule Mexico then? The continuity of the monarchical rule had been shattered, and the colonials owed no allegiance to Spain, solely to the Crown and the Church. This explains the cries of ¡Viva la Independencia! ¡Viva el Rey! Long live Independence! Long live the King!

Now that the King was gone, the demands of Hidalgo and his followers were to drive out the gachupines and confiscate their land; abolish slavery, taxes and the caste system; and initiate an experiment of self-government. The reader must keep in mind, that until then, since early human history, the most stable and widespread form of government had been monarchies. The United States, a most notable exception, had a republican form of government, which was rather unproven for its short longevity, a meager 80 decades. The old consensus among the colonial castes of allegiance to the crown and obedience to its representatives was replaced by a brief unity steered by sheer hatred to peninsulares and sparked among the contending elites and classes by the call to wage a struggle for independence from Spain. Once independence was achieved, this unity was soon marred by the deep inherent divisions among the castes and the ensuing economic chaos. The criollo-mestizo alliance sought empowerment and greater economic participation in prosperous Mexico. Hidalgo—himself a mestizo—was part of this incipient, university trained middle-class. At the heart of the problem was the choice of form of government for the newly independent Mexico, a country of 1,500 square miles and seven million people—comprised mainly of three million Indians, three millions mestizos, one-and-a-half million criollos, and 300,000 mulattos.

The cry for independence unleashed a chain of events: a decade of war, death and destruction, and an economic depression. But also unbound an eager search for a political order and a form of government for Mexico. Once the caste system was abolished, the mestizo-indio population exerted the naked power of their sheer numbers and their willingness to use brute force to attain social and economic gains. No meaningful army could exist without their participation. The adherents of Hidalgo exterminated those running the mining and agricultural sectors and thus crippled the mines and agriculture. As the combatants disrupted the economy, the flow of goods to the cities came to a stand still. The system of public financing and taxes was dismantled as sales taxes and Indian tributes were abolished. The economy was bankrupt and the government, without a new system of public financing in place, had an empty treasury. The Plan de Iguala, a historic agreement among contending factions, was signed on February 24, 1821. It provided for legal equality for criollos-mestizos and peninsulares, independence for Mexico, a Mexican monarchy as the choice of government, and the withdrawal and departure of the Spanish colonial rulers. It also recognized the Church as the preeminent social and religious organization. This agreement was in effect a consensus that the colonial social institutions would remain basically the same, but the Spanish rulers would be replaced by a local criollo elite, comprised of clerics, hacendados, mineros, and traders. Finally, Mexico achieved its independence from Spain on September 27, 1821, and Agustín de Iturbide was installed as a native monarch in 1822. Mexico's government was eventually recognized by France, Great Britain, and the United States. In exchange for recognition, Mexico's new independent government agreed to assume all foreign debts contracted by the colonial government.

The search for an electoral and more representative form of government continued unimpeded. The monarchy of Iturbide lasted one year, and a new constitution that adopted the electoral republican form of government was enacted in 1824. During this period, Mexico underwent political and economic chaos. Internal conflict, division, and confrontation prevailed during this republican experiment, which begot economic collapse and further fostered political instability. One administration was replaced by another; more than thirty leaders became president between 1821 and 1871. Several types of governments were tried, from federal and centralized republic, to dictatorship, to European and native monarchy. There were deep underlying divisions between Liberals and Conservatives. Liberals comprised an incipient middle-class of small rancheros, mineros, artesanos, junior officers, teachers and artists who wanted electoral government and greater participation in the economy, the separation of church and state, the confiscation of church land-holdings, and the secularization of civil ceremonies; in sum they aspired to the political modernization of Mexico and its social and economic institutions. Conservatives, on the other hand, wanted a centralized government, whether a monarchy or a republic, and to revert to pre-independence status-quo of large land-holdings and privileges. They also wanted unity between church and state and recognized the supreme preeminence of the church in civil life. These differences were expressed in political struggles and military clashes and eventually in civil war.

Foreign Intervention and Civil Strife

As peace became more elusive, Mexico fell deeper into anarchy and economic turmoil, and it became an attractive target for foreign powers seeking to profit from its large resources. Northern Mexico received increased attention from the United States which was expressed in greater trade and traffic through the Santa Fe Trail and the Pacific trade route and increased Anglo settlements in Tejas, then part of the Intendencia of Nuevo Santander. Expansionist tendencies emerged from the East coast of the United States, the Manifest Destiny, that foretold the eventual territorial expansion of the United States at the expense of a weakened Mexico.

Once the Louisiana Purchase was accomplished through high pressure tactics-sell it or lose it-in 1803, the United States focused its attention in northern Mexico, and several offers were made to purchase Texas in the 1820s and 1830s. As pressures over its territory mounted, Mexico responded unwisely with more openhanded settlement policies to the extent that Anglo settlers outnumbered Mexicans in Texas by the 1820s. Confrontation leading to a curtailment of the settlements erupted when Anglo Texans refused to obey Mexican law and demanded to operate large-scale slavery-driven plantations. As slavery was illegal in Mexico, the confrontation culminated in the Texas Revolt of 1836 which declared Texas an Independent state. Texas was soon recognized by the United States,

France, and Great Britain. Texas was later annexed to the United Sates in 1844.

In 1838 the French navy commanded by Admiral Charles Baudin shelled the Mexican Golf coast under the pretext that losses by French nationals bad not been indemnified. La Guerra de los Pasteles, as the incident was called, compelled the evacuation of Veracruz and forced payments and reparations to the French by the Mexican government. The event probably convinced France that Mexico was an easy prey to the naked power of the guns. Mexico's main threat, however, as Mexicans painfully would learn years later, did not and would not come from afar or from monarchic tyrants from Europe. The United Sates in 1845 provoked a major conflict with Mexico when President James Knox Polk ordered the United States Army to cross the Nueces River into Mexico and started the Mexican American War. From the outset the United States waged a war of territorial conquest. The Army soon occupied most of Mexico's territory, including Mexico City. in the end Mexico and the United States signed the Treaty of Guadalupe Hidalgo on February 2, 1848 by which Mexico ceded to the United States over fifty percent of its territory.

A new consensus was formed among Liberals, the Plan de Ayutla in 1854, which ended the disastrous leadership of conservative ruler Antonio López de Santa Anna and called for a new constitutional convention that resulted in the liberal constitution of 1857. Ignacio Comonfort was elected President in 1856. He enacted a law to confiscate and sell Church land-holdings. This was an important measure since the Church owned more than fifty percent of the land in Mexico. The law also established a civil registry for births, weddings, and deaths, which would no longer be considered solely religious events but also civil acts. This measure destroyed the ceremonial monopoly Of the Church and took religion out of civil legal life. Comonfort was followed by Benito Juárez, a former Chief Justice of the Supreme Court, who ruled under the new constitution.

A most devastating civil war between Liberals and Conservatives, La Guerra de Tres Años (The Three Year War), also known as La Guerra de la Reforma (The War of Reform), ensued for the next three years. Conservatives, who had been defeated politically earlier, were now also routed militarily in the battlefields. During and after the conflict, Conservatives called overtly upon the French to intervene militarily in Mexico to put an end to a popularly elected government which promoted confiscations of large land-holdings, and the separation between Church and State. Although at first, on the surface, those calls went unheeded, Mexican Conservative elements in Europe initiated schemes for a French intervention with Emperor Napoleon III and his Spanish wife, Empress Eugenia de Montijo.

The misguided idea developed to place the Austrian Archduke Maximilian Von Hapsburg, younger brother of the powerful Emperor Franz Joseph of Austria, and his wife Carlota Amalia (Charlotte Emily) Von Haspsburg as Emperors of Mexico. This was a way for France to secure support from Austria for the invasion of Mexico, and further neutralize any reaction from the United States. The United States, which was preoccupied by internal strife, had to think twice to oppose a consolidated allied European intervention of Mexico.

Although Conservatives hoped that a foreign intervention and a French engineered Austrian Monarchy would re-establish the old system of land-ownership, unity between Church and State, and a centralized form of government-preferably a monarchy-a foreign power needed a "just cause" for intervention and unseating a legitimately elected government. This opportunity would arise when Benito Juárez' government declared a moratorium on the payment of the foreign debt.

The interventionist delusions would make Conservatives oblivious to the people's reaction to foreign threats which, instead, would generate unity and cohesiveness among the Mexican population against a common foreign enemy. It would no longer be a "civil war" but a National commitment to drive out the foreigners of which legends and heroes are made. So it was in Puebla.

The Question of the Foreign Debt

"Pay for troops and for cannons
With which to destroy the people,
From Saligny comes the brandy
And from Jecker the millions."

A verse from "The Austrian's Stanzas of Love," El Cura de Tajamón, El Nuevo Mundo, July 20, 1864

The Batalla de Calpulalpán (Battle of Calpulalpán) on December 22, 1860 marked the military defeat and the end of the Partido Conservador (Conservative Party) as well as the conclusion of the War of Reform. Mexico entered a period of peace a torn country with a virtually destroyed infrastructure and a bankrupt economy due to years of internal hostilities. As Mexico's dawn emerged from political instability, economic collapse, and civil war, the government's treasury was empty, the foreign debt was crippling, and the demand for capital for reconstruction exceeded all viable sources for new capital. The world economy was based on the gold standard and the less estimable, but more plentiful, silver. Mexico was an important producer of silver, and Mexico's government had always been able to use its income from silver receipts as a collateral for domestic and international borrowing. But Mexico's mining industry had declined from decades of neglect, thus the government's room for further borrowing on silver receipts for reconstruction was almost nihil.

Mexico's government was heavily in debt with foreign lenders. Although Mexico had no currency at the time, it issued gold coins, particularly for the international market. A Mexican fifty-peso gold coin was equal to 1.2 ounces of gold. Roughly speaking, the total foreign debt of Mexico then would be equivalent today to $860,000,000 in United States currency, less than a billion dollars. Mexico's debt to England was 69,994,544 pesos of which 16,000,000 pesos was owed to the House of Goldsmith, and 16,000,000 pesos was owed to the House of Barclay; both Houses were from London. Also, 19,298,250 pesos were interest payments in arrears, and the balance were small accounts long overdue.

The foreign debt with Spain amounted to 9,460,986 pesos. The foreign debt with France, contracted with the House of Jecker by the Conservative General Miramón, amounted to 2,084,605 pesos, and as the English Minister Lennox acknowledged at that time, it was insignificant compared with the debt of England.

Benito Juárez promulgated a law on July 17, 1861, declaring a payment moratorium of all domestic and foreign debts for a period of two years. Juárez also informed the foreign and domestic lenders that the government would resume payments "religiously" when better circumstances would allow it. The moratorium was a democratic decision adopted by Congress by 1,112 votes in favor, to 4 votes against. Mexico's government was not reneging the debt; it just wanted more time to get its economic house in order.

The conservative press viciously attacked this decision, but this was only the beginning of the events that would later unfold. The foreign lenders held a convention in London on October 31, 1861 where they agreed to protect the life and property of their nationals and to obtain enforced collection of the debt. Their decision even at that time was so outrageous that it was highly criticized by the world press. The Times of London declared that a simple visit of one frigate would obtain recognition of the English debt and resumption of payment. The New York Tribune quoted Karl Marx's reaction to the news of the planned invasion of Mexico: "...a monstrosity ever recorded in the annals of international history...." Nevertheless, Spain, Britain, and France united behind a platform of enforced collection of debts and prepared for the task of invading Mexico. Mexican reaction to the proposed invasion followed liberal and conservative lines. Liberals opposed foreign intervention as a threat to the newly acquired sovereignty of Mexico.

The Conservatives justified their support for foreign intervention arguing, as the newspaper "La Sociedad" did, "The intervention is not an affront to Mexico, but to its corrupted tyrants,... to the laws of the Reform that legalize vandalism, theft and usurpation of rights and property...." If Mexico was politically weak and economically impoverished by prolonged civil strife, Mexico was also deeply divided. At first it seemed that there wasn't a National consensus against this foreign peril as there had been earlier against the threats of Spain, France, and the United States.

Mexico now demanded a leader more than ever if its very existence and the survival of its electoral republic were to be pre- served. Mexico was worth a battle, and so it was to come.

On the Way to the Front

Spain was the first country to have the troops ready for the invasion of Mexico. General Serrano, Commanding General of Cuba, then still a Spanish possession, prepared three army divisions, who were shipped in 13 frigates and supported by 13 transport ships, all under the command of Marine Commanding General Joaquin Gutiérrez de Ruvalcaba. The composition of the Spanish forces consisted of 5,373 infantry marines, 173 cavalry men, and over 500 support troops such as corp of engineers, bridge builders, and an extensive artillery brigade with fourteen cannons. The total number of troops reached 6,234 men.

The Spanish troops occupied the castle of San Juan de Ultia and the Port of Veracruz on December 17, 1861. Great Britain sent a naval infantry detachment of 700 soldiers and occupied the ports of Veracruz and Tampico on January 6, 1862. On January 8, a French infantry regiment arrived comprised of nine companies, including cavalry, artillery, experienced African Zouaves, and African Escorts (Cazadores).

President Benito Juárez protested against the actions of intervention and called on all Mexicans to "bury the hatred and enmity that had divided us... and unite in defense of a greater and more sacred cause for all men and our people: the defense of the fatherland." On January 9 the plenipotentiaries of the invading countries gave Mexico's government an ultimatum collection or intervention. On January25, 1862, Benito Juárez drew the line and responded, enacting a law condemning to death all invading forces in Mexican territory and their collaborators. His proclamation was short of declaring war.

Juárez, hoping for a last minute diplomatic maneuver that would bring peace, sent General Doblado, his secretary of state, to meet with the invaders at the village of La Soledad. The interventionists designated the Spanish General Juan Prim, Count of Reus and Marquis of Los Castillejos, as their representative. Prim and Doblado met at La Soledad and signed a document known as Los Preliminares de La Soledad [Preliminary (Agreement) of La Soledad], in which the foreign representatives recognized the government of Benito Juárez and the sovereignty and territorial integrity of Mexico; in return the invading troops would be allowed to relocate to Orizaba, Córdoba and Tehuacán. Veracruz at that time was heavily affected by an outbreak of yellow fever, and the foreign troops had increasing casualties without firing or being fired upon. General Prim met later in Veracruz with conservative General Juan Nepomuceno Almonte and other conservative leaders, who had arrived under the protection of the French fleet. Prim soon detected the manipulations between these Mexican conservatives and the French Ambassador Jean Pierre Dubois, Count of Saligny, and the French forces of occupation to establish a French monarchy in Mexico. Commodore Dunlop, the British envoy, was also aware of the French ambitions. In the end, after obtaining assurances of future resumption of payment, the Spanish and British forces left Mexico.

Mexico's government on April 11, 1862 denounced the French maneuver of extending protection to conservative leaders as a direct challenge to the constitutionally elected government and as a violation of the agreements of La Soledad. Doblado wrote, "The constitutional government, the guardian of the Republic, will meet force with force and shall wage war to the end as justice is its cause." The French intentions were clear, but if there were any doubts left, these soon disappeared as sizeable French reinforcements arrived in Veracruz and entered Orizaba on April 20. The French Admiral Julien de la Gravière was replaced by the experienced General Charles Latrille, Count of Lorencez, who had a vast military background in the European theater of the Napoleonic wars. During his 30 years of army service, he had participated in eleven campaigns.

The French troops consisted of one General, 233 officers, 6,348 soldiers, which consisted of three heavy artillery regiments, infantry, marines, two regiments of the feared North African Corps (Cazadores Africanos) and North African Zouaves, and one company of engineers, and 903 horses. The African troops wore blue uniform, as the other French troops, with lily-white turbans. It also included 260 carriages with provisions, comprised of 200,000 individual rations of food and 400,000 of wine. Using the same road that centuries ago Hernán Cortés had used to conquer Old Mexico, the French forces, led by General Latrille, marched toward Mexico City. In its way to the capital city, the center of government, stood the City of Puebla.

Battle of Puebla

The first skirmish before the Battle of Puebla took place near Fortis on April 19, 1862 when Coronel Felix Díaz, also known as El Chato, with a small battalion (Dragones) clashed with a company of African Escorts (Cazadores). The encounter drew an exchange of fire between both sides. Díaz retreated and immediately after he joined General Ignacio Zaragoza, Comandante del Cuerpo del Ejército de Oriente (Commander-In-Chief of the Eastern Army). Ignacio Zaragoza, learning from General Diaz the proximity of the forces, ordered his troops to evacuate Orizaba and continue towards La Ciudad de Puebla.

Upon arrival in Acultzingo, a town before Puebla, Zaragoza instructed Generals Mariano Escobedo and Mariano Rojo and their respective brigades to delay the advances of the Mexican conservative General Leonardo Márquez, who with 7,000 men were in their way to join the French interventionist troops. As the French troops were closing in on Acultzingo, Ignacio

Zaragoza once more ordered the withdrawal of the Mexican forces.

General Latrille, unchallenged, established his headquarters in that city on April 28, 1862. Soon Latrille realized that Zaragoza was withdrawing and would not defend the next positions. As Latrille arrived on April 29 and 30 to the towns of La Caûada de Ixtapa, Cumbres, San Agustín del Palmar, and Quecholac-all on the road to Puebla-he learned that Zaragoza had left those towns one day earlier. Zaragoza arrived at the entrance of La Ciudad de Puebla on May 3, 1862 where he decided to make a stand and defend it.

Upon arrival at Puebla on May 3, 1862, Ignacio Zaragoza learned that the conservative troops of the Generals Leonardo Márquez, Marcelino Cobos, and Ramón Tavera y Taboada now might threaten the southern flank of Puebla. Zaragoza directed General Tomás O'Horan with 4,000 soldiers to encounter the conservative military units 60 miles from Puebla and block their advance. O'Horan's division included the best units of the Mexican cavalry commanded by Generals Rafael Cuéllar and Antonio Carbajal.

Ignacio Zaragoza was born in Goliad, Texas in 1829 and grew up during a tense period of conflict between Mexicans and Anglo settlers; his family had been forced to flee during the Texas Revolt of 1836. He became a teacher and at the outbreak of the War of Reform he joined the liberal militias. During the War of Reform Zaragoza had displayed rare qualities of authority, military sagacity, and strong moral leadership. He had demonstrated his military skills by soundly defeating the superior conservative forces at Silao and later recapturing Guadalajara in 1860. History would give him another responsibility and another test, much more intricate-the defense of Puebla against a well trained, more experienced, and better equipped army. The French army was considered then the best in the world and France, a world power, could not afford anything less.

Ignacio Zaragoza was Comandante dcl Cuerpo de Ejército de Oriente (Commander in Chief of the East Army) which was comprised of three divisions, one infantry brigade, and the cavalry. The East Army had seven generals, 146 senior officers, 932 junior officers and sub-officers, 11,866 troops, 1,272 horses, and 560 mules. This was a large and respectable army. But Zaragoza had deployed the best of his troops to contain the advances of the conservative forces, and he was left to defend Puebla with 4,850 men, including volunteers that were recruited the same day of his arrival in the city. As Zaragoza decided to make a stand at Puebla, he knew well that the smaller size and the inexperience of his troops were his weaknesses.

At dusk of May third, he gathered and addressed his officers: The resistance that this nation of eight million people has so far offered is almost nihil. It is also a shame for this nation that we have this rather small contingent of troops to fight the foreign. enemy. For this reason we must all commit ourselves to die in our positions, because it is not logical to aspire for victory with such a small, ill-equipped army, but we shall inflict the greatest damage....'

Zaragoza then ordered the fortification of Puebla. General Joaquín Colombres, from the corps of engineers, was made responsible to prepare and fortify the defense of Puebla. To build the forts Colombres and his troops reinforced and fortified old churches and colonial estates within the perimeters, but at the periphery of the town they dug trenches and raised obstacles. They built the forts of Loreto and Guadalupe to the north, the forts of San Javier and Santa Anita to the west of the city, and the fort of El Carmen to the south. The day of May Fourth was a furiously active day on both the French and the Mexican sides as they prepared for battle. General Ignacio Zaragoza prepared the battle plan and arranged his forces as follows. General Miguel Negrete, in charge of the 2nd Division comprised of 1,200 men, was ordered to occupy and defend the hills of Loreto and Guadalupe. Negrete in turn assigned General Arratia to defend the Fort of Loreto; General Rojo was given the responsibility to defend the Fort of Guadalupe. Negrete placed in reserve four companies and two small battalions commanded by Coronel Juan N. Méndez, with a total of 300 men. Zaragoza left three infantry brigades of 1,000 men each for various maneuvers, offensive and defensive. The brigades were respectively in charge of General Berriozábal, General Francisco Lamadrid, and General Porfirio Díaz (who much later became president of Mexico). Finally, the cavalry of 500 riders was commanded by General Antonio Álvarez.

Zaragoza addressed all the troops before the battle at the Plaza of San José with these words:

'Soldiers: You have behaved as heroes fighting for the Reform. Your efforts have been crowned by victory, and not just once, but many times you have defeated the enemy. La Loma Alta, Silao, Guadalajara, Calpulaipán are battles that you have made history with your blood. Today you shall fight for something sacred, you shall fight for your Fatherland, and I promise you that this day's journey, some day, will bring you glory. Your foes are the first soldiers of the world, but you are the first Sons of Mexico. They wish to seize your Fatherland. Soldiers! I read victory and faith on your foreheads, Long live Independence! Long live the Fatherland!'

Meanwhile, the French forces spent the night in Amozoc, a town before Puebla, where they prepared themselves for battle. In Amozoc, Latrille learned that Zaragoza had reached and remained at Puebla and was preparing to defend the town in the battle Latrille was anxiously awaiting to demonstrate the superior military skills of his French troops. The Mexican conservative allies, Generals Almonte, Haro, and Tamariz, advised Latrille to attack Puebla by the eastern and southern flanks, thus avoiding the northern fortifications of Loreto and Guadalupe. This advice was militarily sound, but Latrille dismissed it. Latrille firmly believed he had the best forces and military strategists and that there were no serious obstacles to capturing Puebla. A Mexican conservative, Francisco P. Arangois, wrote of this, "The contempt of the French senior officers for the advice of Mexican conservatives has been the cause of many obstacles during the campaign...." These words would prove to be prophetic.

Logic and good military sense convinced Zaragoza that Latrille's forces would attack the eastern side of Puebla, thus he arranged his defenses accordingly. Zaragoza instructed General Miguel Negrete to protect the northern forts of Guadalupe and Loreto. Felipe Berriozábal would support the left flank of Negrete at the foothills of Guadalupe to the barrio Xola. Porfirio Díaz was assigned to cover the eastern roads near Azcárate. General Alvarez' Cavalry would cover the southern flank of Azcárate and provide a right frontline of defense. General Lamadrid would defend the barrio Xola. The Battalion of San Luis, comprised of riflemen, would provide cover to the three infantry brigades' positions previously described. This battle plan was in effect until the morning of May Fifth.

On Cinco de Mayo, at five o'clock in the morning, at the break of dawn in Amozoc, the French troops began their menacing march toward Puebla. They arrived approximately at nine o'clock at the outskirts of Puebla. A vanguard of threatening African Escorts (Cazadores de Africa) with their blue uniforms and white turbans under the command of Colonel Valeze-charged with scouting the terrain and searching for locations to place artillery positions-were constantly harassed by the rifle fire of the Mexican cavalry. In the end Valeze placed three heavy artillery batteries approximately 8,000 feet from Fort Guadalupe to cover the movements of the infantry.

Engraving of the assault on Fort Guadalupe, Puebla, Mexico, by the French Zouaves

On Cinco de Mayo before nine o'clock in the morning, on the Mexican camp, Zaragoza could see the bright sun reflections upon the French bayonets as the enemy came closer and closer to Puebla. He also could see the clouds of dust raised by the 60 raiders of the cavalry battalion of Comandante Martinez who had orders to harass the advancing French infantry. Zaragoza had designed with Martinez' cavalry an advanced warning system. The column of dust made Zaragoza realize that the attack would begin against the fortified hills of Loreto and Guadalupe. This was an indication that Latrille yearned for glory and a sound triumph, which excluded an easy victory. The French General's wish was an arrogant desire, far from a pondered military objective, that would prove to be disastrous. Earlier, on the 26th of April, Latrille had written to the French Minister of War, Marshall Randon, "We possess, over the Mexicans, such superiority of race, organization, discipline, morals and emotions, that I beg your Excellency to inform His Majesty the Emperor that from today, at the head of 6,000 soldiers, I am the Master of all Mexico."

Latrille was ready for battle, but he never contemplated the possibility, nor even less the probability, of defeat at the hands of the Mexicans. His delusion would jeopardize the plans of Napoleon III and in the end would cost him his career in the French Army.

On the French camp, Latrille instructed the First and Second Battalions of African Zouaves, under the direction of Commandants Cousin and Morand, and supported by heavy artillery, to make a frontal assault against Fort Guadalupe. A section of the First Marine Battalion would follow the Zouaves to provide both reinforcement and protection of the right flank from Mexican attacks. Another section of the Second Marine Battalion and Third Battalion would follow next to provide further reinforcements from any other Mexican offensive action. Latrille kept as his reserve a massive force commanded by Coronel L'Heriller comprised of the First and Second Battalion of the 99th Regiment, the Second Battalion of the Third Regiment of Infantry Marines, the First Battalion of African Escorts, and the African Escorts of Vincennes.

As Zaragoza reassessed Latrille's plan of attack, he reorganized the defense of Puebla. General Alvarez' cavalry regiment was placed at the left bound of Guadalupe ready to charge when deemed opportune. However the Lancers of Oaxaca, the Squadron Trujano, and the Lancers of Toluca under the command of Colonel Félix Díaz were left unchanged at the previous position, to the right skirt of Azcárate.

The Battle of Puebla, May 5, 1862 *– This oil painting of the period shows the intitial attack on Puebla de los Angeles (Puebla), May 5, 1862 by the French Army. The fort of Loretto and the fortified monastery of Guadalupe rise in the background of the heights of the Cerro de Guadalupe, and a ridge of high ground dominating the entrance to Puebla, .*

The brigade of General Berriozábal was moved to the left bound of Fort Guadalupe, reinforcing the brigade of General Miguel Negrete, who was covering both forts, Loreto and Guadalupe. General Negrete instructed his troops at the command of General José Manano Rojo to evacuate Loreto and form a line of defense between the two forts and joining forces with Berriozábal troops. General Rojo at the command of the Sixth National Battalion of Puebla was given orders to advance or retreat according to the strength of the French troops.

As the French Zouaves approached Rancho Oropeza at the entrance of Puebla, a cannon shot burst forth from Fort Guadalupe. Its sound swept the hills and valleys of Puebla, hardened the determination of the defenders, and instilled a previously unknown fear in the attackers. The defense of Puebla had begun at eleven o'clock that sunny morning of Cinco de Mayo. As the French invaders arrived at Rancho Oropeza at eleven o'clock in the morning, they went on the offensive.

The assault on the Mexican positions was conducted by a battalion of the Infantry at right flank; at the center between the forts of Loreto and Guadalupe was the First Battalion of Zouaves, and the Second Battalion of Zouaves attacked the Fort of Guadalupe directly. Behind the Zouaves was the First Battalion of Marines. The Sixth Battalion of Puebla engaged the advancing Zouaves and yielded, without ceasing to respond to the fire, and then joined the frontline of defense.

The French troops continued to advance until they were at close range from the Mexican frontline. At the moment when General Negrete lifted his cap as a signal, the firing upon the invaders commenced with great force and rapidity. The French troops were so astounded by the Mexican discharge that they stopped their advance. Emboldened by the pause, the Mexican infantry charged furiously and the French troops retreated for the first time forcing the Zouaves, now without support and reinforcement to depend on, to retreat to their original position.

The French offensive quickly reorganized, received a Battalion of African Escorts as reinforcement, and resumed their attack of Fort Guadalupe. The First Battalion of Zouaves in a heroic effort reached the walls of the Fort. The Second Battalion of Zouaves, the African Escorts, and the Infantry that were supporting the advance of the Zouaves were again repelled by heavy Mexican fire. For a second time the French troops retreated followed in closed pursuit by the infantry of General Berriozábal. The French casualties to that moment had reached 300, including the dead and wounded. Dismayed by the futility of his efforts against the formidable Mexican defenses, General Latrille ordered a counter-attack and, reinforced with the African Escorts of Vincennes, his troops were instructed with the capturing of Guadalupe.

The Victory of Cinco de Mayo. This other oil painting shows the Mexican cavalry with lances picking off the stragglers as the defeated French troops stream back from their failed assault. French troops of the elite 2nd Zouave Regiment, with their distinctive baggy red trousers, are in the foreground. Meanwhile other French infantry, wearing white trousers, blue coats and fezzes, can be seen fleeing in the background.The white gaiters or "spats" over their boots are those troops that General Count de Lorencez had ordered them to freshly whiten for their triumphal march into Puebla.

The Battle of Puebla – *This oil painting of the period shows one of the critical moments of the Cinco de Mayo battle. The French assault has begun to break up under the deadly fire of Mexican marksmen from Fort Loreto and the fortified monastery of Guadalupe. Just then, General Porfirio Díaz appears, leading a detachment of Mexican cavalry in a charge against the dispirited French troops.*

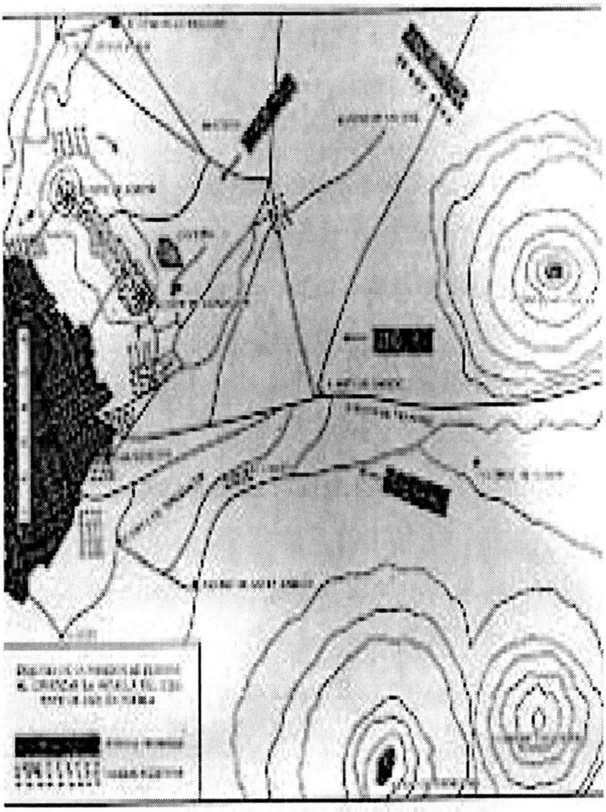

Above, a map showing positions of French (in black boxes) attacking Mexican villagers (indicated by XX's)

On the Mexican camp, General Zaragoza instructed Colonel Lamadrid to send his Battalion Reforma to General Negrete, and his Battalion Zapadores to reinforce the defense of Guadalupe. The third attack against Fort Guadalupe was a fierce joint bid by the Zouaves, the Marines, the Infantry, and the African Escorts of Vincennes. Although some French soldiers managed to escalate the walls of the Fort and engage in hand-to- hand combat with the Mexican defenders, the third assault was as ineffective as the previous ones. Meanwhile Berriozábal halted the advances of the French reinforcements of Zouaves and Marines. At that moment General Negrete ordered a concentrated counter- attack by the Battalion Reforma de San Luis, the troops under General Rojo and the Cavalry under General Alvarez. The French troops for the third time withdrew under heavy fire drawn by Mexican defenses and pursued by the infantry and cavalry. General Lamadrid joined the counter-attack against the Zouaves and Escorts of Vincennes at Guadalupe. General Porfirio Díaz with his Brigade Oaxaca also joined the counter-attack as did Coronel Félix .

The French invaders retreated very quickly to avoid further casualties, pursued by General Díaz who abandoned the quest only 1,000 feet from the French positions. The retreating French forces suffered 482 casualties and the loss of 200 rifles, and Latrille, dispirited and disappointed, ordered a full withdrawal from Puebla. The Mexican forces suffered 250 casualties, including 4 officers and 79 soldiers killed in action, and they expended 190,000 bullets and 2,150 cannon ammunition in their defense.

General Ignacio Zaragoza had been aware from the very beginning that his Mexican forces had to win this battle. The French army was widely acknowledged as the best in the world, and a defeat by them of the Mexican army would have destroyed any hopes for Mexico to repulse the intervention, which commanded a much superior force.

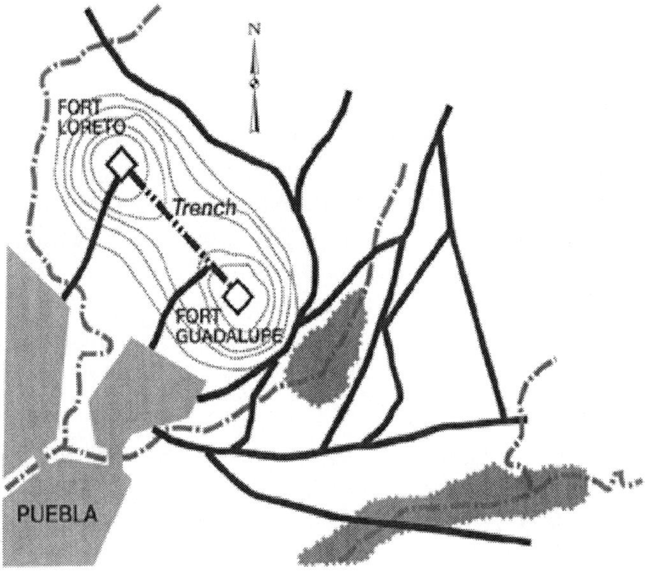

Map indicating the line of trenches dug up by the Mexican defenders of Puebla betwen the Forts of Loreto and Guadalupe.

After the battle, Zaragoza wrote to President Benito Juárez, "The French army has fought gallantly, however its General has acted clumsily.., on this long battle, the Mexican troops never turned their backs to the enemy..."

In the ensuing years of foreign occupation, Cinco de Mayo would become a symbol of a Mexico determined to remain free and the source of strength for Mexicans to fight for National independence, self- determination, and, above all, for Mexico, the fatherland-La Patria! The victory at Puebla had set back Napoleon III's invasion plans for one year, ultimately sending the Emperor's dreams of domination up in the smoke of the Mexican cannons. Not long after his glorious victory at Puebla, General Ignacio Zaragoza, the Tejano hero, became ill and feverish. He died on September 8, 1862 at 33 years of age, four months after the Battle of Puebla, which he so diligently won.. The city of Puebla was renamed in his honor, La Ciudad de Puebla de Zaragoza.

On the first week of July, 1862, the defeated General Latrille was replaced by General Elias Frederic Forey, an experienced commander who fought with Napoleon I at Crimea, Montebello, and Solferino. General Forey landed with fresh reinforcements-some regiments brought from as far away as Indochina (Vietnam)-and in all had at his command a larger force, 30,000 strong. Forey sieged Puebla for several months the following year, 1863. Unable to stand the overwhelming power of the French invasion forces, Puebla finally fell on May 17, 1863.

The Execution of the Emperor Maximilian, 1867 is depiected by E. Manet, *Städtische Kunsthalle, Mannheim; it seems to have been influenced by painting The Third of May, 1808, by Spanish painter Francisco Goya. Manet, the French impressionist painter, allegedly painted this canvas as a criticism of France's involvement in the affairs of Mexico. The political content of this painting inhibited Manet from widely exhibiting the painting.*

The following year, on April 10, 1864, Maximilian von Hapsburg of Austria and his wife

Carlota, in their castle in Miramar near the city of Trieste, Italy, accepted the "throne" of Mexico and began their fateful journey to Mexico. Three years later, in November of 1867, they would return, Carlota conveying the dead body of Maximilian who on June 19, 1867, had been executed by firing squad by Mexican forces loyal to Mexican President Benito Juárez.

"Maximilian, Miramón, and Mejía were awakened on June 19 to a fanfare of bugles and drums. Maximilian asked Miramón: 'Miguel, is this for the execution?' 'I cannot say, Señor," the young general answered, 'as I have not been shot before.' The three were taken to Cerro de las Campanas to be killed by fusilade. Maximilian behaved with great bravery, demanding that Miramón take the place of honor in the center. He gave each soldier in the firing party a gold piece and comforted Mejía at the last moment. Maximilian died like Hidalgo, crying 'Viva Mexíco!' His body....was given back to the Austrians, whose warship waited to bear it home."—From Fire and Blood by T.R. Fehrenbach

Historical Importance of Cinco de Mayo

Many historians have maintained that the main cause of the French invasion of Mexico that led to the Battle of Puebla on May Fifth was the collection of the foreign debt owed to France by Mexico. Since Napoleon III lived considerable time in the United States before taking office in France, he was well aware of the expansionist aims of the United States and its foreign policy to keep Europeans out of the Americas' affairs. Thus, no one has explained the reasons for the French invasion better than Napoleon III, Emperor of France, who wrote to General Forey on July 3, 1862, after the historic Battle of Puebla of 1862:

"There will be persons who will ask you why shall we spend men and money to install an Austrian Prince on a throne. Given the current state of world civilization, the Americas are not indifferent to Europe, because it feeds our industry and commerce. We are interested that the United States of America be prosperous and powerful; but we are not interested that she takes over the Antilles and the Gulf of Mexico, and from there she dominates all of South America, thus becoming the only supplier of products to the New World. Once master of Mexico, Central America and the access to the two oceans (Atlantic and the Pacific), there will not be any other power left but the United States.

...if a stable government is established in Mexico with (the assistance of) the French army, we have placed a dam to the expansion of the

United States.... Therefore... the requirements of our political interests and interests of our industry and commerce, compel us to march over Mexico and establish resolutely our flag, a monarchy, if it is not incompatible with the (Mexican) National sentiments, or at least a government that promises stability."

The French invasion of Mexico, then, was a French response to the Monroe Doctrine, the United States foreign policy that Europeans must stay out of the affairs of the Americas-"America for Americans." The French intervention was a bold and calculated geopolitical move on the part of the French Emperor, who would not yield to the American policy. The invasion was an opportunistic move made possible because the United States was deeply involved in its CIVIL War. The French Intervention was seen as a despicable, callous, calculated way to engage in world affairs not only by Mexicans, the victims of these geopolitical ambitions, but also by many French intellectuals. Victor Hugo, the French literary giant, wrote, "*Mexicans, you are right in believing that I am with you. It is not France who wages a war against you, it is the Empire.... battle, struggle, be terrible, and !f you think that my name may be useful (for your fight), use it. Valiant Mexicans, resist, await; winners or losers, France is with you; is your sister in glory....*"

The Battle of Puebla of Cinco de Mayo of 1862 served as a rallying cry for all Mexicans to oppose foreign intervention and to reaffirm their patriotism. The concept of nationhood had gradually emerged from Independence, through monarchy and civil wars to a republican experiment led by Benito Juárez.

To be Mexican—*ser mexicano*—meant, as it means today, to be a nationalist and oppose foreign domination, to be a republican and oppose absurd elitist (then monarchic) rule, to be a liberal democrat and oppose oligarchic control, and to be self-reliant and struggle for political autonomy and freedom-which would not come easily. Cinco De Mayo was seen as a ray of hope that *lo mexicano*, the Mexican ethos, was not dispensed with but instead was nurtured, devised, and crafted by a united people yearning for liberty: It became a symbol of Mexican resistance and self- determination.

A contemporary view of the Fort Guadalupe. The Battle of Puebla marked one of the most significant episodes in Mexican military history.

Selected Bibliography

1. Berrueto, Ramón Federico. Ignacio Zaragoza. Mexico: Secretaría de Educación Pública, 1966.

2. Cohn Sánchez, Guillermo. Ignacio Zaragoza: Evocación de un héroe. Mexico: Editorial Porrúa, 1963.

3. Echeñique, Rafael. Batalla del Cinco de Mayo de 1862. (Telegramas oficiales relativos a dicha batalla dirigidos a la Secretaría de Guerra. México, Secretaría de Guerra, 1894.)

4. Ignacio Zaragoza, victoria y Muerte, 1862: Selección de documentos relativos a la muerte del General Zaragoza por Francisco López Serrano. Mexico, Comisión Nacional Editorial, PM, 1976.

5. Rosa Perez, José. El General Ignacio Zaragoza..., 1862-1962. (Biografía y cuestiones pedagógicas). Mexico: Editorial Avante, 1962.

6. Lorencez, Guillaume Latrille, Compte de. Souvenirs militaires du General Cte. de Lorencez publies par le Baron Pierr de Bourgoing. Paris, France Emile-Paul, 1902.

7. Olivier, Emilio. La Intervención Francesa y el Imperio de Maximiliano en México. Mexico, Editorial Centenario, 1963.

8. Shefer, Christian. Los Orígenes de la Intervención Francesa en Mexico. Porrúa, 1963.

9. Troncoso P., Francisco de. Diario de las operaciones del Sitio de Puebla. Puebla, México, Editorial Cajica, 1972.

10. Garfias, Luis. La Intervención Francesa en México. Mexico, Panorama, 1985.

11. Gómez-Quiñones, Juan. The formation of Mexican Nationalism.... Encino, California, Floricanto Press, 1992.

Note: This is the most complete Catálogo temático de la historia de las ideas políticas Mexicanas, which provides a most interesting overview of history and political development of Mexican nationalism. As Cinco de Mayo was a military as well as a political act, no other source renders a better understanding of the ideological processes underlying the struggle against the French intervention. We credit Dr. Gómez-Quiñones for that view.

Part II

The Cinco de Mayo in Chicano Poetry

1864-1865

De *El Nuevo Mundo*, San Francisco, 1864-1866. Collected, edited, and translated by Luis A. Torres

The Cinco de Mayo in Chicano Poetry 1864-1865

[These poems are selections from *The World of Early Chicano Poetry, 1846-1910*, Volume I & II, California Poetry, Floricanto Press, 1995.]

The following eleven poems concerning the events and figures surrounding the Cinco de Mayo are originally from the newspaper El Nuevo Mundo, which was published in San Francisco, California between 1864-1866. The dramatic rapidity with which the battle on the Cinco de Mayo became a symbol of pride to the Chicanos in the United States is evident in that these poems were written and published so soon after the event they commemorate. The battle at Puebla was in 1862; eight of these poems were published just two years later in 1864 and the remainder-the three collections of brief poems-in 1865. The Mexicans would not defeat the European powers and their traitorous Mexican allies until 1867. These poems therefore were published during the struggle midway through this exceedingly difficult time for the Mexican republic. Historically these poems served as a mark of solidarity between the poets living in the United States Southwest and the Mexican combatants, including the military forces.

The variety of themes in this poetry reflects the complex artistic milieu of Chicanos during the latter half of the 1 800s. These poems are, variously, patriotic, historical, socially engaged, and satirical. They are deeply committed to the Mexican soldiers; proud of the military leadership of their commanders such as Zaragoza, Negrete, and Rivera; viciously satirical of the triumvirate of Napoleon III, the presumptuous "Emperor" Maximilian, and his wife Carlota; and appreciative of the enduring significance of the events unfolding in Mexico, events to which these poets wished to pay tribute and which they hoped to influence however indirectly.

The range of poetic techniques also suggests that these poets employed their diverse styles and themes in an effort to support in a variety of ways Mexico's struggle for survival as a republic. For example, the epic form of "Oda Patriótica" attempts to chronicle in its resonance the grandeur of the crucial battle at Puebla. The linguistic experimentation of "El Cura Aprendiendo Inglés" with its tri-lingualism of Spanish, French, and English uses Napoleon's own language as a foil to ridicule his protégé Maximilian's cultural veneer. The formal offerings of the "brindis" ("toast") style in the three collections by the patriotic women's clubs solemnize the battles and contract time and distance to place the women on the battlefields where they could more effectively campaign for Mexican victories.

The authors of these poems were all living in the United States Southwest at the time these poems were written although they had close ties with Mexico and many might well have been recent immigrants to the United States. For example, Aurelio Luis Gallardo, author of "Oda Patriótica," alludes in the poem's first line to his recent immigrant status: "¡Un himno de los labios del proscrito!" with the word "proscrito" translatable as "fugitive," "exile," or "refugee." He published three other poems in El Nuevo Mundo including the patriotic "A Mexico" about the Sixteenth of September, Mexican Independence Day.

The poet most represented in this present collection, El Cura de Tamajón (The Priest from Tamajon), published six poems—all included here—in El Nuevo Mundo, each about the Cinco de Mayo, most savage satires about the foreign invaders and the Mexican conservative traitors. The poet A. Ardines, author of "Salve del Austríaco," indicates he wrote the poem expressly to be published in the newspaper ("Para El Nuevo Mundo").

Only one other of his poems was published in El Nuevo Mundo, the lyrical "A María de Los Ángeles" ("To María of Los Ángeles"). Finally, the women in the patriotic clubs are unique in the expression of their poetry in the "brindis" ("toast") form, indicative of the notion that this battle against the foreign invaders and Mexican traitors was a communal effort to be carried out in public forums. I have listed these collections of short poems as three separate units-one of fourteen poems, one of five poems, and one of twelve poems-because each collection refers to a similar theme and because they were published as unified collections in the newspaper.

Special reference should be made here to the collection of five poems from Virginia City, Nevada. Accompanying the poems, published in El Nuevo Mundo May 15, 1865, is an article, dated May 6, 1865, asking for the poems to be published. In the article the women refer to their club as "El Club Patriótico Mejicano" and describe the ceremony they held in Virginia City on May 5, 1865 commemorating the Battle of Puebla of May 5, 1862. The quality of these brief poems suggests that a tangential purpose of this Club-as I believe was also true of the women's Club Zaragoza of Los Angeles—was the creation of such poetry. The varieties of themes and styles in these poems serve as representative reflections of what must have been the universal rejection by the Chicano population against both the foreign invaders of Mexico and their conservative Mexican allies. And the literary quality of these poems is a testament to the aesthetic milieu generated by our Chicano literary ancestors, a testament which can still inspire us today with each celebration of the Cinco de Mayo remembering as we do the battle's purpose, the rejection of the limitations of our freedoms.

Luis A. Torres

Index

El Cinco de Mayo en la Poesía de California, 1864-1865

De El Nuevo Mundo, San Francisco, 1864-1866.

Collected, edited, and translated by Luis A. Torres.

La Oda Patriótica.

Leída en la función con que los mejicanos residentes en San Francisco celebraron el segundo glorioso aniversario del triunfo alcanzado sobre los franceses por el ejército y el pueblo mejicano a las órdenes del intrépido general Ignacio Zaragoza, el 5 de Mayo de 1862. Esta celebración tomó lugar durante el período de La Ocupación Francesa de Mexico como un símbolo de apoyo al pueblo mexicano.

¡Un himno de los labios del proscrito!
En medio de esta pompa,
Resuene precursor del entusiasmo,
Y entre el aplauso audaz, !el aire rompa!
!Lágrimas, fibres y silencio y pasmo,
De evocación le sirvan al recuerdo
De aquel brillante día,
Causa de nuestro orgullo y alegría!
¡Yo el poeta, que cante tal grandeza,
Los nobles hechos de mi patria orgullo,
Sus inmortales triunfos y victorias?
Llevar mi acento a la sublime altura,
Do el águila no sube,
Cruzando audaz la borrascosa nube;
De escrita deja el poderoso rayo,
Del mundo asombro y de Anahuác herencia,
Tu página inmortal. !Cinco de Mayo!

I. Patriotic Ode

Read at the festival with which the Mexican residents of San Francisco celebrated the second glorious anniversary of the triumph over the French by the Mexican people and army under the command of the intrepid General Ignacio Zaragoza, on May 5th, 1862. This celebration took place during the French Occupation of Mexico as a token of support for the Mexican people.

A hymn from the lips of the fugitive!
In the midst of this pageantry,
Resounding precursor to the festivities,
Applause boldly shatters the air!
Tears, flowers, silence and reverence
Serve as evocations to stir our memories
Of that brilliant day,
The cause of our pride and our joy!
Shall I serve as poet to sing such grandeur,
The noble deeds of my proud country,
Her immortal triumphs and victories?
Carry my words to sublime heights
Audaciously crossing tempestuous clouds
Above where eagles can not ascend,
Where lightning bolts leave written, as
Terror to the world, heritage of Anahuác,
Your immortal story. The Fifth of May!

Fiero león que nunca se desbrava,
Que hambriento ruje, y codicioso muerde
Cuanto su garra poderosa alcanza;
Impío rey que en su ambición se pierde,
Y que a la Francia trata como esclava;
Ya sin razón, derecho, ni justicia
A Méjico en sus iras se abalanza
Méjico débil, desangrado, exhausto,
Apresta ya sus águilas guerreras.
Que Dios le da valor y confianza.
¡Y un hombre, sólo un hombre
Que el árbitro se llama de la Europa,
Que la estremece a su menor antojo,
Con el orgullo de su nombre ordena,
Y a miles de hombres bárbaro condena
Al destierro, a la muerte!
Napoleón tercero
Aliado vil de la facción traidora,
A Méjico en mala hora
Provocara a la lid astuto y fiero.
¡Ese hombre no es la Francia!
Ella the noble, poderosa y grande;
Era el cerebro de la vieja Europa,
La f uente del progreso;
Fué como Grecia y Roma,
Como la Albión altiva,
La que meció la libertad del mundo,
¡La enemiga mortal del retroceso!

Fierce lion which is never tamed,
Who roars in hunger, and greedily mauls
All that his powerful claws can reach;
Impious king, victim of his own ambition,
Who treats France like a slave;
Now, without reason, right, or justice
He rushes into Mexico in his fury;
Mexico, weakened, bloodied, exhausted,
Yet prepare your eagle warriors.
God grant you valor and confidence.
And one man, just one man,
Called arbiter of Europe which
Trembles at his smallest caprice,
Commands the former glory of his name
And barbarously condemns thousands
Of men to banishment, and to death!
Napoleon the Third,
Vile ally of the traitorous faction,
Cunningly provokes fierce conflict
With Mexico in its weakest hour.
That man is not France!
She was noble, powerful, and grand;
She was the light of ancient Europe,
The fountain of progress;
She was like Greece and Rome,
Like haughty England,
Which sowed liberty throughout the world,
The mortal enemy of cultural decline!

Mas ahora en la abyección del servilismo
Con falsas glorias sustituir pretende
La libertad que su amo le escatima;
Tras de empresas gigantes,
Triunfos soñando bellos y distantes,
Nación guerrera fía al Océano,
Herto imprudente en su avidez de gloria,
Naves que al continente americano
Su honor como a un sepulcro inmenso llevan:
Sus playas tocan, y al llegar las huellan
Sus orgullosos, bélicos soldados:
Al clima tropical horror lo cobran,
La ardiente zona su arrogancia abate,
Y por favor nos piden,
Salir de nuestras costas sin combate
A más templada zona;
En el honor fiando, que él adora,
Méjico generoso
El pacto admite que el francés abona,
¡Y esbirros de ese vil que los envía,
Su fé al romper, con cínica arrogancia,
Faltos de honor y faltos de bidalgula,
Dan al honor de Francia
La Soledad por tumba y epitafio!
Avanzan ya sus bélicas legiones,
Por la áspera montaña y la llanura
Adelantan sus trenes y cañones,
Y al fin tras rudo batallar sangriento,
En que fatiga la metralla al viento,
En las gloriosas cumbres de Acultzingo
Diezmados son sus bravos batallones.

But now in our abject servility
He professes to supplant false glories
For the liberty his master strips from us;
Following grandiose designs,
Dreaming of triumphs, distant and beautiful,
The warlike nation lords over the Ocean
And in its foolish greed for glory gluts
Its ships like giant sepulchers to come to
Try their honor in our American continent:
They touch our beaches and their proud,
Warlike soldiers tread upon the shore;
The tropical climate causes them dread,
The sweltering sun dulls their arrogance,
And soon they plead with us to grant them
Leave of our shores without a battle
To escape to a more temperate zone;
Trusting in honor, which he adores,
Generous Mexico
Grants the pact the French propose,
But myrmidons, envoys of their vile leader,
Destroy Mexico's faith with cynical arrogance;
Lacking honor and lacking nobility,
They give to the honor of France
But Solitude as both tomb and epitaph!
And now they advance their warlike legions,
They march their retinue and their cannons
Over rugged mountains and across prairies,
And finally, after fierce and bloody battle,
In which the cry of steel wearied the wind,
The brave battalions are decimated
On the glorious summits of Mount Acultzingo.

De nuevo en Puebla estrepitosa zumba
Mortífera metralla:
¡Ay! !Cuántos héroes hallarán su tumba
En esa ardiente y desigual batalla!
La lucha crece con furor insano
Que atiza airado el genio de la guerra,
Su fuego asombra, su fragor aterra
Al esclavo servil, no al mejicano
Que por su patria y por su honor pelea.
Chispas lanzando de sangrienta lumbre
Se cruzan las caladas bayonetas,
La tierra se enrojece, el humo estiende
Su espesa nube, ronco centellea
El bárbaro canón, la muerte siembra
En la brava y revuelta muchedumbre
Que ardiendo en ira el triunfo se disputa
Ora en el llano ó la fragosa cumbre.
Rompen el aire las alegres dianas,
Infantes y jinetes se revuelven,
Y entre blasfemias, gritos y amenazas
Vencidos ellos las espaldas vuelven.
¡Re1inchando en la fuga los corceles
Alzan nubes de polvo en su camino,
Y de la tarde a las postreras luces
Los franceses do quier riegan las cruces
De Crimea, Magenta y Solferino!
Guerreros vencedores de la Europa,
¿Quién espantó sus águilas triunfales?
¿Quién los ataja, here y desordena?
¿Quién con fuerza invencible los destroza?
¡Los hijos son del pueblo que acaudillan
Berriozábal, Negrete y Zaragoza!

Suddenly in Puebla the clamor resounds
Of the death-dealing machine-gun:
Oh! how many heroes will meet their tombs
In that ferocious and unequal battle!
The fight swells with insane fury
Wrathfully inciting the genius of war;
His fire astounds, his tumult entombs
The servile slave, but not the Mexican who
Fights for country and his country's honor.
Sparks dart from bloody fire,
Warriors cross soaking bayonets,
The earth turns red, smoke spreads
Its dense cloud, barbarous cannon
Flash out hoarsely, death is sown
Among the brave and furious multitude
Burning in wrath as victory is disputed
On the plains as on the tumultuous summit.
Trumpets calling retreat pierce the air,
Infantry and cavalry turn swiftly
Hurling blasphemies, cries and threats as,
Defeated, they turn their backs to the battle.
In their flight, the whinnying battle-horses
Raise up clouds of dust in their wake, and
From afternoon to the last glimmer of sunlight
The French in disarray scatter the crosses
Won in Crimea, Magenta and Solferino!
Warriors! Victors of Europe!
Who now has dismayed your triumphant eagles?
Who shames them, torments them and unnerves them?
Who with a force invincible destroys them?
The victors are sons of those they command,
Berriozábal, Negrete, and Zaragoza!

¡Día inmortal! ¡Sagrado monumento!
¡Bendito el sol que te alumbró propicio!
Y, !benditos los héroes que a la tumba
Viste bajar! Que siempre te bendigan
Todas las almas grandes,
Todos los generosos corazones
De las demás naciones
Los pueblos de la América que alumbra
El sol de la divina democracia
Sabrante bendecir, !Patria querida!
Que en esa lucha, sin flaquear en ella,
¡Venciste a la primer nación de Europa!
Occidental estrella!
¡Invencible amazona!
¡Admiración del mundo en tu desgracia!
Tu nombre brille al fin de zona a zona,
Vuelve a grabar en láminas de oro,
Vengadora al vibrar tu ardiente rayo,
Otro Dia de gloria,
Que ensalse tu decoro,

Immortal day! Sacred monument!
Blessed the sun which propitiously lighted
Your way! Blessed the heroes you saw
Sink into their tombs! May the great
Souls always bless you,
All the generous hearts
Of all other nations,
The people of America
Lighted by the sun of divine democracy
They wisely exalted, Oh beloved country!
For in that battle, undaunted,
You defeated the first nation of Europe!
Western star!
Invincible amazon!
The admiration of the world in your
misfortune!
At last your name shines from sea to sea,
Now the tale will be forged in gold
engraving,
Avenging nation, of when your raging fury
was
Stirred into another day of glory,
Exalting your honor,

!Otro grande, inmortal, Cinco de Mayo!
!Oh! bella patria mía
Tu afrenta en sangre de traidores lava,
Y antes te cubran tus airados mares,
o tus volcanes con hirviente lava,
!Y así la tumba de los libres seas
Que no la esclava de La Europa esclava!
!Señora tú de medio continente
No has menester de otra imperial corona,
Que la que el Hacedor del Universo
Puso en la Libertad sobre tu frente,
Y un pueblo grande que de ti blasona!
!Gloria a la libertad, luz de la ciencia!
!Paso al progreso, redención del mundo!
Y hoy que nuestra alma con su triunfo goza
Juremos por el héroe Zaragoza,
!Progreso, Libertad, Independencia!

Aurelio Luis Gallardo
El Nuevo Mundo, San Francisco 5 de Mayo de 1864
[Nota editorial: Publicado 28 de Julio de 1864.]

Another grand, immortal Fifth of May!
Oh! my beautiful country,
Wash this affront in the blood of traitors.
Rather you would be sunk by wrathful seas
Or covered by a volcano's boiling lava
Than become slave to enslaved Europe!
Rather become the tomb of the free!
Oh Mistress, at the heart of the continent,
You have no need of any other imperial crown
But that which the Creator of the Universe
Placed with Liberty upon your head,
And a glorious populace which boasts of you!
Glory to liberty, light of knowledge!
The path of progress, redemption of the world!
Today as our hearts rejoice your triumph,
We pledge, by the hero Zaragoza,
Progress, Liberty, Independence!

Aurelio Luis Gallardo
El Nuevo Mundo, San Francisco May5, 1864
[Editor's Note: Published June 28, 1864.]

II. A La Gentil Carlota

Tiene Carlota gentil,
Talle esbelto, risa grata,
Un aliento de pensil...
Una mirada que mata,
El cabello mas sutil...
-!Y la pata?.....
Dicen que verla enamora,
Y que el alma se dilata
Cuando entre rayos de aurora
Se ye su frente de plata
Con la gracia seductora,
!Y la pata?.......
Dicen que le oyó Aguilar,
Coplero de Miramar,
En la voz una sonata
Que ni la misma Traviata
Se le puede comparar.....
!Y la pata?....
El Pájaro la retrata:
No es nariguda, no Chata,
Y doy fé de su hermosura,
Del tocado a la cintura,
-!Y1apata?.......

II. To the Elegant Carlota

Elegant Carlota, graced with
A lovely figure, a gentle laugh,
A breath as from a meadow,
A look that steals one's heart,
Hair that is infinitely fine...
Ah, but her foot?
They say one loves her on sight
And that one's soul expands
When, in the early light of dawn,
One sees her lustrous image
And her perfumed grace and charm...
Ah, but her foot?
They say she inspired even Aguilar,
Feeble balladeer of Miramar, to hear
A sweet sonata in her voice
With which not even La Traviata
Can hope to compare...
Ah, but her foot?
The great Pájaro does her portrait;
Her nose is perfectly proportioned,
And I swear faithfully to her beauty
From her coiffure to her waist...
Ah, but her foot?

Es hermosura barata,
Su vestido es una bata:
Y su chicote en la mano
Para el pueblo mejicano,
Que le está diciendo: ¡Ingrata!
-!Y la pata!...
Por ella Gregorio Mier
Está su juicio a perder,
Y Barrera se remata;
El mismo Anievas y Liata
Dice'..."Perfecta mujer".....
-!Y la pata!
Le adora la Mojigata,
Y la nobleza pasquata
Parodiándola la imita,
Solo mi hermosa mulata
Dice....será muy bonita,
-¿Y la pata?
Pasé....la gente se agrupa,
Una especie de Chalupa
Que en prora inmensa remata
Saca, y la nsa desata...
Ese es el zapato.....¡¡Chupa!!
-¿Y la pata?

It is a cheap beauty,
Her clothes, a ragged wrap:
The riding whip she carries
Is intended for the Mexicans
To whom she cries: "Ungrateful!"
Ah, but her foot?
Because of her Gregorio Mier
Is going to lose his trial,
And Barrera, his verdict;
And likewise Anievas and Liata
Say... "Such perfection in a woman!"
Ah, but her foot?
The hypocrites love her,
And the dimwit nobility parody
Her, as she mimics them,
But that lovely brown darling
Says... she must be lovely,
Ah, but her foot?
She passed... the people gathered,
A small canoe appears, from
The immense prow an extremity
Is raised, and laughter explodes...
That canoe is her shoe...! Indeed...!
Ah, but her foot[7]...

Piececito mejicano
Que en el guante de una mano
Hallar pudiera alpargata:
Dile a la Austríaca insensata,
Qué quepas aquí....no es llano,
-¿Y La pata?......
Tiene a Luzbel su pié frito,
Y que es pata de chivito..
Segün mi nana relata.
Aunque su alma *innamorata*
Se nos semeje infinito......
-¿Y la pata?.....
Pudiera caber, Carlota,
Toda tú en una bellota,
Tras de la hoja de una mata,
Bajo la piel de una rata,
Con crinolina y capota...
¿Y la pata?

El Cura de Tamajón
El Nuevo Mundo, San Francisco
27 de Julio de 1864

Tiny little Mexican foot
Which fits in the glove of a hand
As in a sandal: tell that
Senseless Austrian what you
Have here...is not barren,
Ah, but her foot!
She has Lucifer's foot fried
Brown and toasty-she says it's a goat's
Foot, or at least so says my grandma.
And even if her soul is enchanting
And it appears to be infinite...
Ah, but her foot9
If you could fit, Carlota,
Entirely inside an acorn shell,
And had a leaf of a plant as a roof,
And covered yourself with rats' fur,
And with horsehair and thistles...
Ah, but her foot!

The Priest of Tamajón
El Nuevo Mundo, San Francisco,
July27, 1864

III. Décimas Amarosas del Austríaco

"Tú me quisiste, aquí vengo
México, que por mí abogas.....
Vengo a tus brazos sin drogas
Y hasta mis pobres mantengo.
Preguntas, a que me atengo,
Silencio, infeliz nación:
Cual bardo de corazón
Traigo en mi nave velera,
Una voluntad sincera,
Lealtad y buena intención.
"De la suerte por favor
Me hallo de manos a boca,
Con un trono que me toca
Como a un eunuco el amor."
Napoleon grita: valor,
Que éstos mis caprichos son,
¡Y qué llevo a esa nación!...
-Rapazuelo, aguarda, espera.....
-Una voluntad sincera,
Lealtad y buena intención.
"Paga trenes y cañones
Con que destroce la gente,
De Saligni el aguardiente
Y de Jecker los millones."

III. The Austrian's Stanzas of Love

"You wanted me, so here I come,
Mexico, for you pleaded for me....
I come to your arms free of debts, and
I will feed and clothe even the poor."
"You ask on what I lay my
Hopes, silent, forlorn nation:
And which bard of the heart
I bring in my pilgrim ship,
A sincere benevolence,
Loyalty and good intentions.
"As luck would have it
I suddenly found myself endowed
With a throne, as due to me
As a eunuch is due love."
Napoleon cries: "Courage,
For such are my capricious whims,
And what shall I give that nation?..
Little kid, save, and wait..
A sincere benevolence,
Loyalty and good intentions."
"Pay for troops and for cannons
With which to destroy the people,
From Saligni comes the brandy
And from Jecker the millions."

Forja francos a montones;
Los aztecas ricos son,
Y a cada contribución
Pon en la austríaca bandera:
Una voluntad sincera,
Lealtad y buena intención.
"Así la misma rutina,
Tuve yo de trovador
Al encarecer mi amor
De escribiente de oficina.
"No tenía ni esclavina,
Ni en el bolsillo un tostón:
Mas la nupcial bendición
Pedí mi capital era
Una voluntad sincera,
Lealtad y buena intencion."
"Aztecas, haced caminos,
Aztecas, abrid canales,
Las mejoras materiales
Dan pesetas y destinos.
¿Y qué no dáis tres cominos
Para esta negociación?...
Ya doy tres cosas que son:
Tres Californias, ¡frio1era!
Una voluntad sincera,
Lealtad y buena intención."

He counterfeits piles of Francs;
The Aztecs are wealthy,
And with each contribution they
Further weave the Austrian flag:
A sincere benevolence,
Loyalty and good intentions.
"And in the same manner
I served as a troubadour,
To sell dear my love songs
Of a scribe in my position."
"I didn't even own the shirt on
My back, nor a dime in my pocket:
Yet I asked for a nuptial blessing:
My only inheritance was
A sincere benevolence,
Loyalty and good intentions."
"Aztecs, build the roads,
Aztecs, dig the canals,
The best materials are worth
Nickels and dimes, and destiny."
And won't you give three
Mustard seeds for this affair')...
I will give three things:
Three Califomias! Trifles!
A sincere benevolence,
Loyalty and good intentions."

Y ni una hoja de tabaco:
A probar fortuna viene....
¿Pues sabe usted que este nene
Es más que tonto, bellaco?...
¿Qué arriesga el virtuoso austríaco?
Pescarse mas de un millón,
Y en la menor rebelión
Saldrá por cualquier tronera,
Esa voluntad sincera,
La lealtad y la intención.

El Cura de Tamajón
El Nuevo Mundo, San Francisco
20 de Julio de 1864

And not even a tobacco leaf:
He comes to savor his fortune........
Don't you see this child
Is not just a fool, he's a villain?...
What does this virtuous Austrian risk?
To pocket more than a million,
And upon the smallest rebellion
He will sneak out of the nearest rathole,
A sincere benevolence,
Loyalty and good intentions.

The Priest of Tamajon
El Nuevo Mundo, San Francisco
July20, 1864

IV. A Los Prestamistas de Maximiliano
Soneto

Sacad, sacad las libras esterlinas,
Banqueros de marqueses y de lores,
Que se arruinan, si no, los acreedores
Del gran monarca de las manos finas.
Ya os consigno de Mexico las minas,
¿Quién duda que vendrán tiempos mejores
Y que será el primor de los primores,
Quien viene a edificar sobre ruinas?
Gran monarca es aquél, que al coronarse
Necesite dinero de prestado,
Como el indio infeliz para casarse:
¿Qué importa? se verá mas endrogado,
Y si quiebra, no habrá de quién quejarse,
Que está la penitencia en el pecado.

El Cura de Tamajón
El Nuevo Mundo, San Francisco
21 de Julio de 1864

IV. To Maximilian's Pawnbrokers
Sonnet

Bring out, yes, bring out your bank cheques,
You bankers to princes and to kings, that you
May ruin yourselves-and how !-you creditors
To the Grand Monarch of the elegant hands.
He has consigned Mexico's mines to you;
Who doubts better times will come for you,
Times which shall be the grandest of the grand,
For you who come to build among our ruins?
Great is this Monarch who to crown his
Coronation must borrow from your largesse, like
The unfortunate Indian must borrow to marry:
What does it matter? He will plunge deeper
Into debt and, if he goes broke, he can grieve
To no one, for his penance is in his sin.

The Priest of Tamajon
El Nuevo Mundo, San Francisco
July21, 1864

V. En La Sentida y Tardía Muerte del Dr.. Francisco J. Miranda

Elegía

Tuve a mis pies postrada a la fortuna
Y traje del copete mi cordura
A la calva ocasión al estricote.
Cervantes.
Venid moscos, chacales, zopilotes!
Sauces llorones, fúnebres cipreses;
Gatas austríacas, cárabos franceses,
Ancianas de bigotes,
Sepultureros, parcas gemidoras,
Y de lechuzas quejumbrosa banda,
Y en coro funeral lloremos juntos
¡¡¡La gran traición!!!, pasóse a los difuntos,
¡Ay de nosotros! el Doctor Miranda.

V. On the Deeply Touching and Late Death of Dr. Francisco J. Miranda.

An Elegy

I had fortune prostrated at my feet and
The aristocracy's apparel was my discretion
At the fair which lacked both rule and order.
Cervantes
Come mosquitoes, jackals, buzzards,
Weeping willows, funereal cypresses;
Austrian pussy-cats, French setters,
The aged with dragging beards,
Grave-diggers, the wailing Fates,
And bands of mournful owls,
And in a funeral chorus we shall lament
Of this great treason, Woe to us! that
Doctor Miranda has crossed the river of death.

¡Quién pudo imaginar que tan travieso,
Tan vivo, tan chistoso,
Con tal sagacidad y tanto seso,
Se le ocurriera el pensamiento ocioso
De largarse al imperio de los muertos!
¿No ha sido éste el mayor de los entuertos?
¿Quién correrá desde poniente á oriente,
Con gracioso disfraz de carbonero,
Llevando al retortero
A la mas refinada policía?
Lloremos ¡ay en tan menguado día!
¿Quién puede reemplazar tanta destreza,
Ni aquella actividad mas que de ardilla,
Ni su fecunda y pícara cabeza?
Era del sansculote pesadilla: *
Mercurio de roquete y solideo,
Maquiavelo de turca o de sotana,
Que por zurrarle a Juárez la badana,
Hubiera ido a las aguas de Leteo.
Más que columna, fué polín de S alas,
El ídolo del Clero,
Su Pegaso, su Fígaro, su Palas.
Sin el prosaico antojo de morirse,
Hoy fuera el confesor de la devota
Emperatriz Carlota:
Y habría llegado a ser si no se escapa
Patriarca, Obispo, Cardenal y Papa.

* “sansculote”: Francés, “sans-culotte.” “Nombre que dieron los aristócratas en Francia, en 1789, a los revolucionarios que sustituyeron el calzón corto por el pantalón... sinónimo de patriota.” *Pequeño Larousse Ilustrado.*

Who could imagine that one so shrewd,
So witty, so mischievous, with
Such sagacity and such brains,
Could ever conceive such a useless notion
As to journey to the kingdom of the dead!
Is not this the supreme iniquity?
Who now will fly from west to east,
Wearing the foolish disguise of a coal-miner,
Deceiving with false hopes even
Those with refined good breeding?
We weep, Oh! on such an ominous day!
Who can ever replace his prowess,
His adroitness, of a squirrel,
His fertile and crafty mind?
He was a nightmare to the ragged rabble: *
A Mercury to the clergy's surplices and caps,
Machiavelli of drunkenness and floggings,
Who to give Juarez a whipping would
Have journeyed through the waters of Lethe.
More than the pillar, he was the mortar
For Salas, and the idol of the clergy,
Their Pegasus, their Figaro, their Pallas.
But for his prosaic caprice of dying,
Today he would serve as confessor
To the devoted empress Carlota;
But for his departing, he would become
Patriarch, Bishop, Cardinal, and Pope.

In the Spanish version, "sansculote" is the original word "sans-culotte," "the name the French aristocrats in 1789 gave to the revolutionaries who substituted shorts for pants [culottes]...synonymous with 'patriot." Pequeño Larousse Ilus. [Trans. mine].

A su lado, Pelagio era un enano,
Barajas una triste chuchería,
Un átomo Mungía,
Feto de un mes, el célebre Sollano,
Y el padre Covarrubias un bendito,
Que junto al gran Miranda valía un pito.
Mas ¡ay! aconteciόle lo que al loco
Que le tocó la grande en un billete:
Cobró la lotería,
Que fué de su existencia el solo antojo,
Y tuvo tal ecceso de alegría
Que al tocar las talegas cerró el ojo.
La aurora se eclipsó de un hemisferio,
La hoguera se apagó, la luminaria
De toda la manada reaccionaria,
¡Llorad! ¡llorad! ¡Oh momias del imperio!

El Cura de Tamajón
El Nuevo Mundo, San Francisco
24 de Julio de 1864

Compared with him, Pelagius was a dwarf,
Barajas a sad trifle,
Mungia a mere atom,
The celebrated Sollano, a month-old fetus,
And Father Covarrubias a simpleton,
A mere trifle next to the great Miranda.
And it came to pass that this lunatic
Hit the lottery jackpot with his ticket:
He took up his winnings,
The lone dream of his existence,
And felt such excessive joy that
Upon touching the purse, his eyes closed.
This hemisphere's aurora has been eclipsed,
The bonfire has expired, this luminary
Of the entire reactionary herd-
Weep! Weep! oh mummies of the Empire!

The Priest of Tamajón
El Nuevo Mundo, San Francisco
July 24, 1864

VI. El Cura Aprendiendo inglés

The Yankee Dul
Poned cortinas,
Pronto, Monsieur,
Mi gola blanca,
Mi traje azul,
Viva el imperio,
Me ahogo ¡ay Jesus!
-Yo no te entende,
Dijo el atún.
(Que era un Yankazo
Como abedul.
Con cada pata
Como un almud)..
Vieca..¿no danzas?
Zi Yankee dul?

VI. The Priest Learning English

The Yankee Doodle
"Hang up the drapes,
Hurry, Monsieur,
My white epaulet,
My blue suit,
Long Live the Empire!
Oh Jesus! I am choking!"
"I can't understand you,"
The idiot said.
(He was a huge Yankee,
Big as an oak,
Each foot
Half an acre in size.)
"Old lady.... Will you dance?
The Yankee Doodle?"

Ensayen danzas
De aire andaluz,
Salas gritaba
Con inquietud,
-Mas ronco acento,
Le dijo chust,
(Era el yancote)
No haya rum, rum,
Ensayen todos
Zi Yankee dul.
Señor Austriaco,
¿Qué bailas tü?
(¿Serán enanos?
¿Será Mambrü?
¿Bailas Mazurca...
¿Bailas? ¿No hay mus?
Baila un Palomo
Con Padedú,
Te hará la Algara
Currucutú,
-O un bailecito
Bailará yoú....
Que es de mi tierra..
Zi Yankee dul.

"Rehearse dances
Of an Andalusian flair,"
Monsieur Salas
Nervously hollered.
But a hoarse accent
Told him "hush,"
(It was the huge Yankee)
"No time for la-di-da.
Everyone, rehearse
The Yankee Doodle."
Austrian lord,
What do you dance?
Dances for dwarves?
Do you dance the Mambrú?
Do you dance the Mazurca?...
Will you dance at all?
Will we daily in the salon?
Dance a Palomo
With a Pas De Deux,
The Algara will make you
Currucutu,
Or will you dance
This little dance...
One from my country....
The Yankee Doodle?

¡O que bonito!
Cuánta inquietud
Y hermosa orquesta
Que es el non plus.
Mas la dirije
Lincoln y puf
En vez del Sacra
-Y en vez de augus
Tos nobles.....acentos,
¿Qué es? ¡¡¡Patapıum!!!
Toca Paniagua
Zi Yankee dul!!!

Con qué atacabas
A O'Donojú
!Traidor Almonte!
¿Que también tú
Le haces al Austria
La portabá ?....
Barres lacayo,
Tinta de pús
Tronos sainetes
Resté sans cu
Abajo......y dancen
Zi Yankee dul.

El Cura de Tamajón
El Nuevo Mundo, San Francisco
29deJuliode 1864

Oh how lovely!
What a clamor your
Lovely orchestra plays,
Most disconcerting.
For it is directed by
Lincoln, thank God!
Instead of the
Sacred Coronation
And instead of the sacrosanct
... sounds,
What is it? Footstomping!!!
Good buddies, will you play
The Yankee Doodle!!!
With what did you attack
O'Donoju, you
Traitorous Almonte!
Will you too
Make a mouthpiece
of Austria7..
Lackey, color
These farcical thrones
Yellow like pus.
You'll end up
With nothing where you
Sit on your throne
Below.., and all will dance
The Yankee doodle.

The Priest of Tamajon
El Nuevo Mundo, San Francisco
July29, 1864

VII. Horas Serias del Cura

¡Oh! no llaméis feliz la águila presa
Porque el oro en su cárcel reververa.
Dejadla sola recorrer la esfera,
Perdiéndose en el sol
¡Oh! no llaméis feliz la palma enana
Que encierra el invernáculo opulento;
Dejad que su abanico tienda al viento,
¡Burlando su furor!
!Ay no envidiéis la suerte del salvaje
Que esclavo escucha del jardín la fuente,
Dejadle su llanura y su torrente,
Sus cierras y su aduar!
¿Por qué sobre del pueblo arrojas flores
Al ver que su tirano toca el puerto...
Cuando grita la patria ¡el pueblo ha
muerto!
¿Murió la libertad?
Yo lo siento; del látigo el chasquido
Hizo en los vientos del amago alarde,
Y la traicion gritó: ¡pueblo cobarde!
¡Viva el emperador!

VII. The Priest's Serious Hour

Oh! Don't say the imprisoned eagle is happy
Just because the gold in his cell glitters. *
Leave him to himself to survey the heavens
And lose himself in the sun.
Oh! Don't call the rosebush happy
Enclosed in the opulent greenhouse;
Let its blooms unfold to the wind,
Mocking its fury!
Oh, don't envy the enslaved savage's fate
As he listens to the garden's fountain,
Leave him his meadows and his streams,
His huts and his villages!
Why do you toss flowers at the people
When we see tyranny knocks at the door....
When the nation cries, "The people have
died!
Is liberty dead?"
I feel it; the whip's bitter crack made
At the sound of your threatening boast,
While treason cried: "Cowardly people!
Long live the Emperor!"

* [The eagle is the main symbol of the Mexican flag. It was also the term for the Mexican twenty-dollar gold piece.]

¡Viva,! que con sangre de tus hijos
Será purpúreo el manto de tus reyes,
¡¡Oh pueblo de rodillas!! que tus leyes
Las dicta ¡Napole6n!
De rodillas ¡oh pueblo! que tu frente
Que bañó con sus lindos resplandores
El sol indeficiente de Dolores,
Inclínese servil.
Y cortesanas prostituídas clamen:
En medio de los reales regocijos,
Levantando en sus brazos a sus hijos:
¡¡¡Viva la emperatriz!!!

El Cura de Tamajón
El Nuevo Mundo, San Francisco,
3OdeJuliode 1864

Long may he live! For your kings' mantles
Shall be stained with your children's blood,
Oh! country on bent knees! for your laws
Are dictated by Napoleon!
On your knees, Oh my people! Your proud heads,
Bathed once with the lovely resplendence
Of the enduring sun of Dolores, **
Now must servilely bow.
And in the midst of the royal merriment,
Lifting their children overhead in salute,
Prostituted courtesans cry,
"Long live the Empress! !!"

The Priest of Tamajon
El Nuevo Mundo, San Francisco
July30, 1864
** [A reference to the town of Dolores, in west central Mexico, where Father Hidalgo on September 16, 1810 sounded the famous battle cry for independence that began the Mexican Revolution against Spanish rule.]

VIII. Salve del Austríaco.

Para "*El Nuevo Mundo.*"

Que Dios te salves archiduque,
Leal por antonomasia;
Carlota, llena de gracia
Dios salve tu devoción!
Porque si hoy es con vosotros
El Bonaparte bastardo,
También se halla ese petardo,
Que se llama "rebelión."
Tal vez os contáis seguros
En el trono mejicano,
Porque os bendijo la mano
De otro bendito impostor;
¡Mas cuidado! que el azteca
Despreciará esa impostura,
Al rechazar la criatura
De un tirano usurpador.

VIII. A Hail Mary for the Austrian.

For "*El Nuevo Mundo.*"
May the Lord grant you salvation,
Archduke, as your title is truly given;
Carlota, full of grace, may God
Grant salvation to your devotion:
For today if that bastard
Bonaparte is with us, that
Explosive called "rebellion"
Also lurks within our midst.
Surely you think yourselves
Secure upon the Mexican throne,
For blessed art thou by the hand
Of another blessed impostor;
But beware! for the Aztecs
Will despise that impostor
And denounce the disciple
Of the tyrannical usurper.

¿De qué os servirá el apoyo
De Francia y otros poderes
Si solo entre las mujeres!
Os harán juntos volar?......
Los mejicanos leales
Os pondrán presto de luto,
Aunque esté bendito el fruto,
Y su vientre de ultramar...
Los apóstatas traidores
Con el, bando de Jesús,
Vo1arán tras de su cruz
A hundirse en Jerusalén;
Y en el mejicano cielo,
Limpio ya de ese nublado,
Se leerá de luz rodeado:
¡Salváse La patria, amén!

A. Ardines.

El Nuevo Mundo, San Francisco
17 de Agosto de 1864

What good will the support
Of France and other allies serve
If you force to flee only
Those united among women?..
The loyal Mexicans will
Quickly make you mourn,
Even if blessed is the fruit
Of thy womb, you aliens....
The traitorous apostates
With the proclamation of Jesus
Will fly after their cross
To hide away in Jerusalem
And in the Mexican sky,
Wiped clean of storm clouds,
Will be written in radiant light:
"Our country is delivered from evil, Amen!"

A. Ardines

El Nuevo Mundo, San Francisco
August 17, 1864

IX (Héroes del Cinco de Mayo]

(En esta edición del periódico, se dice que había un club en Los Angeles, Club Patriótico Mejicano de Zaragoza de Señoras de Los Angeles. Estas Señoras escribieron los siguientes poemas.)

1.
Méjico libre ha de ser
Pese al francés insolente.
Esto mi instinto presente
Si sabemos sostener
Nuestro digno presidente.
Con heroísmo defended
Donde quiera que te hallares
De nuestra patria los lores;
Y en su entusiasmo Merced
Brinda por Benito Juárez.

Merced J. de Gonzáles

IX (Héroes of Cinco de Mayo]

[In this edition of the newspaper there is an article about the Zaragoza Patriotic Mexican Women's Club of Los Angeles. The women in this club authored the following poems. The article immediately precedes the following fourteen untitled poems, each in the form of a "brindis," or a "toast," all about the Fifth of May commemoration celebrating the victory by Mexican forces under the direction of General Zaragoza over the French army of invasion in 1862.

1.
My heart tells me
Mexico will be free
Despite the arrogant French,
If we know how to assist
Our worthy president.
With heroism we should defend
The leaders of our country
Wherever we might be;
And Merced in her enthusiasm
Gives a Hail! to Benito Juárez.

Merced J. de Gonzáles

2.
Por el héroe de Oajaca
Dueño de mis simpatías.
Aquel que por todas vías
A los franceses ataca,
Brindo por Porfirio Díaz.
Rosario Díaz

3.
¿Qué hombre será el más villano?
Maximiliano.
¿Y cuál será el mas bribón?
Napoleón.
Dios con una maldición
Los confunda a los abismos,
Y allí con los diablos mismos
Propongan en intervención,
Brindo por su destrucción.
Andrea Belarde

4.
Pesqueira y García Morales,
Los baluartes de Sonora;
Genios que mi pecho adora:
Brindo por los dos iguales,
Por Pesqucira y por Cachora.

Sebastiana Chacón.

2.
To the hero of Oaxaca,
He who has my sympathies,
He who in all possible ways
Has attacked the French,
¡Hai1! to Porfirio Díaz.
Rosario Diaz
3.
Which man is the greatest villain?
Maximilian.
And who is the most evil one?
Napoleon.
But God has redeemed our nation
And sent them both to damnation,
And this, their eternal perdition,
Is their reward for intervention
They brought for our destruction.
Andrea Belarde.
4.
Pesqueria and Garcia Morales,
The bulwarks of Sonora;
Geniuses my heart adores:
I Hail! to both equally,
For Pesqueria and for Cachora.

Sebastiana Chacon.

5.
Con constancia y con valor
Sigues la sacra tarea;
Siempre la patria te yea
Combatiendo al invasor.
Por Patoni brinda Andrea.
Andrea Sáenz
6.
Viva el héroe de Guerrero
Y nunca Maximiliano,
Viva el liberal ufano
Y muera el infame clero,
Brindo por Altamirano.
Francisca Fernandez
7.
A todo el Norte ver quiero
Libre, fuerte, independiente;
Quiero verlo prepotente,
Y con gusto placentero
Brindo por el presidente.
Bell Warner

5.
With devotion and with valor
You pursue your sacred task;
The country will forever see you
In combat against the invader.
Andrea hails Patoni.
Andrea Sáenz
6.
Long live the hero of Guenero,
And death to Maximilian;
Long live the proud liberator
And death to the infamous clergy;
I give a Hail! to Altamirano.
Francisca Fernández
7.
I long to see all the North
Free, strong, and independent;
I long to see a mighty power
Full of happiness and joy;
I give a Hail! to our President.
Bell Warner

8.
Que su fama siempre aumente
Del mundo en todo el espacio;
Es mas fino que un topacio.
Brindo por ese valiente,
Brindo por Riva Palacio.
Andrea Sáenz
9.
Con valor y con constancia
Le haces la guerra al bonete;
Con la espada y gabinete
Haces temblar a la Francia
Brindo por Miguel Negrete.
Concepción Alaníz
10.
De la patria éres fanal
De los traidores terror,
Al francés causas horror
Como tú no hay otro igual,
Por ti brindo Carbajal.
Hilaria Rendón

8.
May his fame forever flourish
Through the world's wide breadth;
His fame is purer than topaz.
I give a Hail! to this valiant man,
I give a Hail! to Riva Palacio.
Andrea Saenz
9.
With valor and with devotion
You wage war against the fortress;
With your spear and your council
You force the once-bold French to fear.
I give a Hail! to Miguel Negrete.
Concepción Alaníz
10.
You are a beacon to our country,
To traitors' hearts a terror;
Your name to the French is horror,
And like you there is no other;
A Hail! to you, Carbajal.
Hilaria Rendón

11.
Yo no quiero monarquía,
Yo no quiero aristocracia;
Ni del traidor la palacia,
Quiero ver La patria mÍa
Libre de toda desgracia.
Aroadia Alvarado
12.
El tonto Maximiliano
Y su consorte Carlota
Al buen sentido derrota
Por que el hombre es un marrano
Y su mujer una idiota.
De conformidad ese dúo
Gobiérnese a los traidores,
A frailes y aduladores,
Sin mas talento que un búho.
Refujio Díaz

11.
I reject their monarchy,
I reject aristocracy;
I reject a traitor's palace;
I accept this and nothing less:
My country free from all disgrace.
Aroadia Alvarado

12.
That stupid Maximilian
And his consort Carlota
Have shattered all true reason
Because the man is a pig
And his woman is an idiot.
In a union of peers those two
May govern the traitors,
Friars, and adulators,
With no more talent than an owl.
Refujio Diaz

13.
¡Méjico! tú que en tus Campos
El sol de mi vida ví,
Cuna do yo me mecí
De juveniles encantos.
Tü que en el bosque moviente
De tus perfumadas brizas
Gocé las dulces delicias
De su divino ambiente.
Quisiera hacer con mi vida
Tu ventura.
Con cuánto amor y temura
La diera, patria querida
Y que fueras grande y fuerte
En el mundo
Y que el universo inerte
Te admirara absorto, mudo.
Francisca García
14.
Mis amigos una copa,
En honor de los valientes
Que cubriendo estan sus frentes
Con laureles de victoria.
Por que la pelea no envano,
Sea tan tenaz tan terrible
Que a su frente estruendo, horrible

13.
Mexico! You in whose countryside
I saw the frst light of my life,
The cradle where I was lulled
in my youthful enchantments.
You in whose forests swaying
With your perfumed breezes
I rejoiced in sweet delights
Of your divine environs.
I long to weave my life
Into your fortune.
With such love and tenderness
I give my life to you, dear country,
I long to see you great and strong
Throughout the world,
And may the inert universe
Gaze upon you silent and amazed.
Francisca GarcÍa
14.
My friends, I give a toast
In honor of the valiant ones
Whose heads are wreathed
In laurels of sweet victory.
Know your struggle is not in vain,
Be it ever so cruel and fierce,
For we will resound together,

¡Se muera Maximiliano!
Refujio Díaz
El Nuevo Mundo,
San Francisco
29 de Marzo de 1865

"Maximilian soon will die!"
Refujio Diaz
El Nuevo Mundo,
San Francisco
March 29, 1865

X. (El Cinco de Mayo]

[Cinco poemas de Virginia City, Nevada, celebrando el 5 de Mayo.]

1.

La causa por que mi patria
Se encuentre hoy en agonías,
Son los mismos mejicanos
Que han tornado simpatías
A esos infames tiranos.
Brindo por Porfirio Díaz!
Da. Agapita Gonzáles

2.

Invito a los concurrentes
A que con voz melodiosa,
Brindemos por Zaragoza
Y por todos sus valientes.

Da. Teresa Contreras

X. (On the Cinco de Mayo)

[These untitled poems, all by women, celebrate the Fifth of May, 1864, when Mexican forces under General Zaragoza defeated the invading French military forces at the Battle of Puebla. According to a letter from Virginia City, Nevada preceding the poems, these were written by "the members which constitute the board of the Patriotic Club of Mexico" of Virginia City. They were read "at the ceremony held on the Fifth of May, a date solemnized by all patriotic Mexican men and women of this city...." Translation mine.]

1.

The reason that my country
Today finds itself in agony
Is that some Mexicans accepted money
To validate the French tyranny.
But to he who has freed us,
All Hail! to Porfirio Díaz!
Doña Agapita Gonzales

2.

I invite all here to rejoice
And sing in a melodious voice
To Zaragoza and his valiant men
A mighty Hail! once again.

Doña Teresa Contreras

3.
Méjico, perla preciosa,
Hoy te ves asesinada
Por esa Francia orgullosa
Que a su ejército venció
El inmortal Zaragoza.
Da. Julia Ortiz

4.
¿Quién mandó a Méjico la intervención?
El perjuro Napoleón.
¿Quién nos quiere gobernar?
Fernando el de Miramar.
Pues se puede retirar
Este archiduque simplón,
Que su trono ha de estallar
En la boca de un cañón.
¡Brindo por la independencia de nuestra nación!
Da. Silveria Luna

3.
Mexico, our pearl so precious,
Today that French usurper
Tried to steal you from us,
But Zaragoza was the victor
And immortal lives among us.
Doña Julia Ortiz

4.
Who forced on Mexico this intervention?
The perjured Napoleon.
Who seeks to rule us from afar?
Fernando of Miraniar.
But we will rebuke
This simpleton Archduke:
We will explode his throne
With the mouth of a cannon.
Hail to our independent nation!

Doña Silveria Luna

5.
El trono que Napoleón
Presento a Maximiliano
Se lo dió con condición
De que ofreciera a su hermano
Que sobarían con baldón
El tesoro mejicano.
¡Brindo por nuestra nación!

Da. Carmen Gonzáles

El Nuevo Mundo, San Francisco, 15 de Mayo de 1865

5.
The throne that Napoleon
Presented to Maximilian
He gave on the condition
That as a gift to his brother
To inflate his evil reputation
Would be given Mexico's treasure;
But I cry Hail! to our nation!

Doña Carmen Gonzalez

El Nuevo Mundo, San Francisco, May 15, 1865

XI. (Homenajes de gratitud]

[Nota editorial: Los siguientes párrafos y los doce poemas, son "brindis," en homenaje a oficiales, especialmente Rivera, Herrera y Medina, que lucharon en La batalla de Puebla y quienes fueron prisioneros de Maximiliano. Da. Merced J. de Gonzáıez, Presidenta del Club Zaragoza:

Dos años hace que celebrábamos los triunfos adquiridos por nuestros valientes hermanos sobre los "primeros soldados del mundo", que con tanta injusticia invadían nuestro suelo; y hoy tributamos un debido homenaje de gratitud a los señores Rivera, Herrera y Medina, tres oficiales pertenecientes al ejército de Oriente. Ellos pertenecieron a aquel valiente ejército que con tanto denuedo defendió el honor nacional. Nosotras, al hacer las justas apreciaciones del mérito adquirido en los dias de prueba, no hacemos m!s que cumplir en parte con nuestro deber. Y silos débiles servicios emanados de nuestro patriotismo fueren alguna vez útiles a la patria, en ese dia serán coronados los deseos de todas las buenas mejicanas residentes en esta ciudad.

Brindo, pues, por los defensores de nuestra santa causa; por los que, despreciando las amenazas y promesas del déspota francés, han preferido los más grandes sufrimientos, a las halagadoras seducciones de la traición. Los siguientes son los brindis que recordamos:

XI. (Homages of Gratitude]

[Editorial note: The twelve short poems each in the form of a "brindis" or "toast," pertain to military officials, including Rivera, Herrera, and Medina, who led battles against the French invaders and were imprisoned by Maximilian. By Merced J. de Gonzales, President of the Zaragoza Club .

It has been two years since we celebrated the triumphs achieved by our valiant brothers over the "first soldiers of the world," who with such injustice invaded our land; and today we pay tribute as a debt of homage of gratitude to Rivera, Herrera and Medina, the three officials from the Eastern battles. In valiant battle they courageously defended our national honor.

We women, to show just appreciation of the merit these men won in those trying days, do not do more than pay our debt in part. And if these humble services which emanate from our patriotism can help our country in the future, on that day these wishes of the good Mexican women residents of this city would truly be crowned.

I give a Hail!, then, to the defenders of our sacred cause, for those who, scorning the threats and promises of the despotic French, have preferred the greatest sufferings to the extravagant seductions of treason.

The following are the Hails! we have offered:

1.
A los tres ex-prisioneros
Rivera, Herrera y Medina,
Con placer mi alma se inclina
Por valientes y guerreros.

Francesca Roldán

2.
Con alegría placentera
Y de todo corazón,
Brindaré en esta ocasión
Por el capitán Herrera.

Exiquia Acevedo

3.
Dichoso el que sacrifica
Por la patria su existencia,
Y que con toda su influencia
A la guerra se dedica
Con todo su ser y esencia!

Rosario Díaz de Reihm

1.
To the three ex-prisoners
Rivera, Herrera, and Medina,
My soul reaches out with joy
To these, our valiant warriors.

Francesca Roldán

2.
With joyful happiness
My heart goes out again
To honor and to bless
Herrera, our great Captain.

Exiquia Acevedo

3.
Happy is he whose existence
He will give to save his country,
And with his utmost influence
Fights to see his nation free
With all his soul and essence!

Rosario Díaz de Reihm

4.
Cuando el infame francés
En San Pedro combatió,
En el momento encontró
De la fortuna un revés
Y su fama se acabó.
Doy mi amor al que defiende
De su patria los umbrales;
Por el valiente Rosales
Mi pecho en fuego se enciende.
!Que vivan los liberales!

Isabel Warner

5.
Do quier la fama pregona
Tus hazañas y valor;
Adquiriste grande honor,
Valientísimo Corona.
Por ti brindo con amor.

Andrea de Sáenz.

4.
When the French, to their shame,
In San Pedro came to war,
In one moment they did deplore
How their glory came to blame,
And their fame was gone forevermore.
I give my love to he who did defend
His country in its time of need;
To valiant Rosales for his noble deed
My bosom's fire to him I send;
May our liberators always succeed!

Isabel Warner

5.
Your fame has come from above,
Your heroic feats and valor;
You have won eternal honor;
Valiant Corona I Hail! with love!

Andrea de Saenz

6.
Brindo con todo placer
Por el Club de Zaragoza;
Porque cumple aquel deber
Que sólo puede caber
En una alma generosa.

Isabel Ramírez

7.
Con todo el placer que siento
Brindo por esos valientes,
Que no mancharon sus frentes
Con indigno juramento,
De su patria estando ausentes.

Mariquita Ramírez

8.
Yo brindo por la constancia
Que supieron mantener
Los emigrados de Francia.

Andrea Velarde

6.
I give a toast with all my heart
For the honor of the Zaragoza Club;
For I repay the debt we owe
Which can only be contained
Within the most generous soul.

Isabel Ranifrez

7.
With all the joy I can feel
I cry Hail! to the valiant,
Those who did not stain their
Honor with an unworthy oath,
Never failing their country's need.

Mariquita Ramirez

8.
I honor those who were so wise
To leave the tyranny of France;
Its loss of freedom they despise.

Andrea Velarde

9.
¿Por qué, Méjico hermoso,
Mi relicario amado,
La plant a del malvado
Te pisa presuroso?
Mas detengan su carrera
De su jefe los esclavos,
Pues todavía tenemos bravos
Como el capitán Herrera;
Brindo por que nunca muera.

Teresa Morales

10.
Oigo el aire como suena
Y entre los árboles trina,
Recomendando a Medina
Por su valor y su pena.
Brindo porque al regresar,
Haga al invasor temblar.

Concepción de García

9.
Tell me, lovely Mexico,
My reliquary of love,
Why does that malicious one
In arrogance tread on you?
Though slaves have helped the
Cause of their master Maximilian,
We do not lack for noble soldiers,
Like Herrera, our noble Captain;
I Hail! that his fame may never die.

Teresa Morales

10.
I listen how the breezes sound
As they trill among the trees,
Commending brave Medina
For his labor and his valor.
On his return I bid him honor,
For he made the invader tremble.

Concepción de García

11.
En medio de la tarde
Parece que cruzaba
Un ángel que cantaba:
¡O muerte o libertad!
Mas esto es realidad;
Y la reunion ent era
Lo contemplara en Rivera.

Refugio Arce de Silva

12.
En la antigua Roma habla
De Vesta, templo formado,
Do por mujeres cuidado,
Perenne se mantenía
Constante el fuego sagrado.
Las socias de "Zaragoza"
A las de Vest a imitando,
El fuego patrio atizando,
Con inquietud afanosa
La lámpara estan cuidando.

Filomeno Ibarra
El Nuevo Mundo, San Francisco
21 de Julio de 1865

11.
In the middle of the evening
I thought I saw an angel
Crossing past and singing:
"Either Death or Liberty."
But that was not a vision;
The entire congregation
Had gazed upon Rivera.

Refugio Arce de Silva

12.
In ancient Rome there stood
A temple built to Vesta,
Tended all by women, and
Its constant sacred flame
Was kept perpetually burning.
Now the members of "Zaragoza"
Following the rules of Vesta
Keep our country's fire bright
And with painstaking pride
Take constant care of our lamp.

Filomeno Ibarra
El Nuevo Mundo, San Francisco
July 21, 1865

Printed in the United States
113423LV00003B/28-63/P

9 781888 205053